The Money Manual

A Realistic Money Guide to Helping You Succeed
On Your Financial Journey

TONYA RAPLEY
OF MY FAB FINANCE

This book is dedicated to my mother, Sharon Rapley, my sister, Nicole, my late mother in-law, Marcia Banton, my late Grandmother, Sarah Jackson, and all the powerful women who showed me what is possible and inspired me to own my power.

Table of Contents

To get the most out of this book download your
companion Money Manual workbook at
MyFabFinance.com/TheMoneyManualWorkbook

Foreword

I haven't always had it together. To be honest, I don't always have it together. But I have learned if you understand what you need to do to get back on track, you can always get back on track.

A lot of times we become aware of how financially unstable we are because an event or experience jolts us, revealing our financial deficits.

The problem most people have is they don't know where to start. Whether experiencing joblessness, divorce, a medical emergency, or dealing with negligence, most people don't know how to pick up the pieces once they embark on their financial journey.

I started My Fab Finance in 2013 after deciding enough was enough. I stopped acting like my finances would autocorrect themselves, and I became proactive about improving my financial situation, and ultimately my life.

Every day, I'm approached by people who ask the important question, "Where Do I Start?" This book is a simple guide created to help you start now, with what you have.

Whether you're a recent graduate, newly divorced, or have just decided a few things have to change, I am assuming that you have purchased this book to steer your life down the path of financial security.

I want to commend you for taking a big courageous step forward. But, I also want to remind you that while beginning this journey is important, finishing this journey is also important.

In our age of social media and hyper connectivity, people have become obsessed with making declarations of their intentions, without doing the work needed to follow through.

In this book, you will find the financial basics. I do not cover investing in this book because I don't specialize in investing. I dibble and dabble, but I understand my limitations and work with an advisor for my major investments, only investing money I can afford to lose when I do it on my own.

I do not cover building a business in this book. I want to focus on helping you build your financial foundation, and in a perfect world, your foundation would be established and strong before you could create a business. While businesses can transform your finances and your life, often business fail after only a few years of operation because the owner encounters financial issues due to the lack of a solid financial foundation.

A business can't save you from poor financial behaviors.

Thank you for allowing me to be a part of your journey.

May this book serve you beyond your expectations.

Now, let's get to work.

Chapter 1

Conducting Your Financial Self-Assessment

I often read books and articles that reveal the "habits of the highly successful." Typical habits include waking up early (not for me), reading the newspaper or a book, exercising daily, or some other seemingly beneficial habit that people with means and success should have the time for.

One of the most helpful practices I often see overlooked is self-checkups. A self-checkup, in the non-physical sense, means investigating areas of your life to identify what is and isn't working for you. As creatures of habit, we often commit ourselves to things, people, and practices that do not have a place on our journey.

In starting your financial journey, begin with an assessment of where you are so you can get to where you want to be. An assessment is not meant to shame you, nor should it be a tool for gloating. Your assessment should be used to provide you with guidelines and structure so you can determine what needs to be done to help you become the best version of yourself.

During this chapter, I will walk you through how to do a simple self–checkup.

Getting started is one of the most challenging aspects of going on this financial journey. I can almost guarantee it won't be the only challenging aspect, but determining where to begin is often one of the biggest hurdles. Where you are helps you see where you need to focus your attention in order to get things going in the right direction. This part of the journey is essentially the lacing of your sneakers for the marathon before getting into the race. Unlike a running course, most of us don't have a clearly indicated start line.

I want to extend a word of caution here because when you are prompted to take action, your knee-jerk reaction may be to start at the point that gives you the most stress; however, your stress might simply be a symptom of an underlying issue, such as living above your means or failing to properly plan out your budget and expenses.

I encourage you to dig deeper and complete the questions (on the next two pages) even if they make you uncomfortable. In order to determine the actual problem, not the symptoms, you have to ask yourself a few questions based on the following:

1. Where you are
2. Where you want to go
3. The resources you have available to help you get to where you want to go

Need more space? Visit www.MyFabFinance.com/MoneyManualWorkbook to download your free PDF and see all of the activities in this book in one place.

Assessing Where You Are

I'm sure when you read that headline a few adjectives came to mind.

Anxious
Doubtful
Confused
Excited
Optimistic

Maybe you're feeling all those emotions at once.

Everyone is at a different starting point on their journey because everyone has unique life experiences and resources. My younger sister and I were raised in the same house with the same parents. We have a lot of similarities. We are both driven and independent, and we understand the importance building on our parents' legacy. But we are still very different. I'm the unpredictable

Gemini child who excels in social settings, and my sister is the calculated Capricorn who values her privacy. Our personality differences led us to make unique choices affecting our financial journeys. Just because someone is raised in the same household as you, employed by the same employer as you, or earns the same salary as you, doesn't mean they will have a similar journey as you.

During the exercises in this chapter, you may realize that you have feelings of pain or disappointment when it comes to money because they are seeded in comparison.

I encourage you to explore those feelings and seek to create the best possible outcome for you, based on everything that has lent to the evolution of the person you are today.

TO DETERMINE WHERE YOU ARE, THERE ARE A FEW QUESTIONS YOU SHOULD ASK YOURSELF:

In my life right now, what is going well in relation to my money?

What is not going well in relation to my money?

Are there any current emergencies relative to my finances that I need to address?

Are there any upcoming life events that could potentially impact my financial situation (good or bad)?

What financial goals would I like to accomplish over the next year?

Next Five Years?

Next Ten Years?

What is my credit score?

How much debt do I have?

Is my job secure?

Assessing Where You Are

Am I happy at my job, or do I see myself transitioning in the near future?

Who depends on me financially?

When it comes to my money, what gives me anxiety or keeps me awake at night?

What is my biggest financial fear?

Why do I have this financial fear?

Review your responses and look for similarities or themes. Does fear, or feelings based in fear, continuously come up? Does ambition peak through? Are there any items that brought happiness to you and put a smile on your face?

It is common for people to list—with ease—what is not going right in their lives when it comes to money; nevertheless, honing in on what is going right for someone financially is just as important to recognize. If you had more negative than positive, I want you to fill out the gratitude map in the Money Manual Workbook.

I don't have the answers for you. You have the answers for you. This is your journey; I'm just here to help you understand the steps you need to take to achieve your desired outcome.

When you understand where you are, it is easier to determine what you need to do and move along your journey.

Where You Want to Go

Have you ever thought about something you wanted, but saying you wanted it (or accomplished it) just felt different? That's because there's a difference between hoping something happens and planning for it to happen.

Unplanned events happen every day, but our desires become more powerful and take on a life of their own when we proclaim them as ours.

During this section, we will create your goals.

Before we get started though, I have a confession to make.

I am not a fan of creating S.M.A.R.T. goals. My eyes literally roll when a presenter or trainer pulls up the slide and begins to walk people through the process.

If you aren't familiar with S.M.A.R.T. goals (lucky you), it's a goal-setting process widely used by trainers and educators with the goal of helping people establish better goals and reach said goals by ensuring they are: specific, measurable, attainable, relevant, and time bound.

An example:

Regular goal: "I want to pay down my debt this year."

S.M.A.R.T. goal: "I want to pay off all of my credit cards (with debt totaling $8,500) in the next six months using money from my performance bonus, tax return, and side hustle."

You're probably like, that goal is specific as hell and feels super clear, Tonya. What could you possibly have against S.M.A.R.T. goals?

My issue with S.M.A.R.T. goals is they lack (1) a why and (2) accountability. Declaring what you want to do and when you want to do it isn't enough. Also, I find S.M.A.R.T. goals boring. They don't excite me, and often, they don't excite my clients. It's not until we tap into what excites us about goals that the fire is ignited.

So, what do I suggest in place of S.M.A.R.T. goals? I suggest S.I.T.A. goals.

S.I.T.A. (yes, I made this up) is an acronym for goals that are: specific, intentional, have a timeline, and hold you accountable.

Specifics: So, while I strongly dislike the word specifics (because hate is an ugly word), I believe specificity is indeed important. Stating exactly what you want to do helps differentiate where you are from where you want to be.

Specific doesn't have to mean, I'm going to transfer money to my savings at 8:46 a.m. on payday. It could mean, I'm going to save money before I spend a dime, when I get paid on the 1st and the 15th.

Intentional: Everything begins with intention. After this step, your goal becomes bigger than just a thought; it is defined by your WHY. It's what makes your goal personal— helping you connect with what this goal means to you and why you want to achieve it. You may find that your why is your greatest motivator.

You can say, "I want to buy a multi-family home in Chicago" as a why. But a deeper connection (or why) would be, "My entire family was raised in this community, and I've realized that if I don't buy property in the neighborhood I call home, I won't be able to afford to live here due to rising rent. It's time to become a landlord instead of a renter so that I can control my housing costs. Buying not only allows me to remain here, but it also allows me to begin creating assets not liabilities while building on the legacy I'll leave behind."

Now, you can't tell me you didn't get excited reading that intentional statement.

Timeline: I didn't say S.M.A.R.T. goals were all bad, and what I do like about them is they encourage you determine what the finished product looks like and when you would like to arrive at the finish line.

We've all had or been witness to goals that never end. It is often argued college degrees are no longer required to prove you have the skills to do the job, but they do demonstrate you have the ability to finish projects you start. I can't be the only one who has landed a job thinking they required a degree for this?

The more flexible you are with your expectations for attaining your goals, the less likely you are to achieve them. By setting a goal expiration date, you give yourself a personal deadline.

Accountability: In Scott Belsky's book, Making Ideas Happen: Overcoming the Obstacles Between Vision and Reality, the author states, "Accountability...binds you to the relentless pursuit of our goals." There are goals I had accountability partners for and did not complete, but I felt awkward as hell talking to them or admitting I didn't do what I said I would do.

Most humans don't fear failure, we fear public failure. When you establish an accountability (partner) for your goal—and are forced to explain why you did not achieve that goal—it becomes a lot more difficult to abandon your goal or make decisions counterproductive to that goal.

In writing this book, I enlisted the support of an accountability partner who was also working to finish her book (shout out to Jessica.) Jessica showed up every day asking me how things were coming along with the book. She did this to the point that I got tired of making vapid excuses and tapped back into the reasons why I wanted to write this book.

It's because of my accountability partner that you are reading this book today.

Your accountability partner can be your spouse, your best friend, a coach, an entire mastermind group, or even your child. Everyone is not cut out to be your accountability partner, however. You should choose someone who has the time to hold you accountable, someone who is not impressed by your excuses, and/or someone who will not allow you to be the mediocre, comfortable version of yourself (which is easy to default to).

And, that's the S.I.T.A. process for establishing goals.

I'll be honest. This book was a S.I.T.A. goal. I am a part of a professional speakers' mastermind group. We meet twice a month virtually to discuss business development strategies. During this time, we also share resources, tolls, and opportunities, and support one another in our businesses through our online forum. During our New Year meeting in January 2017, I set a goal to write a nonfiction book by December 31, 2017, among other goals. And then, other exciting projects came along, and this book was shelved. That is, until a member of my mastermind group held me accountable.

It is my hope that creating goals for your financial journey will give you a perceived finish line—a celebration zone (because what's progress without having at least one opportunity to celebrate).

You can begin to audit your actions and ideas based on how aligned they are with your goals. For example, if your goal is to eliminate debt, ask yourself if the purchase under consideration is bringing you closer to paying off debt or not.

Use the SITA formula worksheets on the next pages to specify at least two financial goals you would like to accomplish within one month, three months, six months, and a year of reading this book.

*Here's an example of one of my goals
using the S.I.T.A. standard:*

Specifics: Pay off the remaining $2,272 of my South Carolina Student Loan my mother took out for me during my undergraduate studies

Intention: This will bring me one step closer to being debt free, and I want to be debt free by the age of 35. I am also tired of my mother asking me about this loan, and I don't want to have any debt that affects her.

Timeline: No later than May 2018

Accountability: My mother (I might regret that)

Now, it's your turn.

Specifics:

Intention:

Timeline:

Accountability:

The S.I.T.A. Standard

Specifics:

Intention:

Timeline:

Accountability:

Specifics:

Intention:

Timeline:

Accountability:

The S.I.T.A. Standard

Specifics:

Intention:

Timeline:

Accountability:

Resources You Have Available to You

If you are reading this book, you have been given a privilege.

Before you assume I'm going all Kanye on you and saying it is a privilege to read my words, let me explain.

In 2015, I had the opportunity to travel to Ghana. No experience in my life has forced me to confront my privileges the way this trip did. I suddenly realized how much I took for granted: reliable electricity, hot water for showers, access to education, healthcare, and the ability to easily access tools and information on creating a business via the internet.

If you are reading this book, you have access to education— which is a privilege not afforded to millions across the globe.

I open this section discussing privilege because we often assume if we don't have a certain amount of money or belong to a certain family, then we don't have privilege among our resources. And while the level of privilege may determine the amount of resources available to you and the ease of accessing those resources, it doesn't mean you don't have resources to support you along your journey.

So far, we've identified where you are and where you

would like to be, but what you have available to help you get there is also important.

You already have a resource available to you in this book, but the additional resources to help you along your financial journey can be broken down into three categories.

My coach, Jullien Gordon, breaks our resources down into three categories, which I believe are applicable to many areas of our lives.

Personal Resources

This journey starts, depends on, and ends with you. What are your strengths? Do you have access to tools to help you make more money so you can achieve your goals faster? What are your past successes which ensure you are successful on this financial journey?

Social Resources

Who do you know that can help you with your goals? Do you have a friend who is really disciplined and can support you? Is there someone to whom you can vent your frustrations? Is there someone who will share resources with you and help you along your journey because they can see your vision?

Financial Resources

It's a lot easier to manage money when you have it coming in. Your financial resources can come in the form of income, job opportunities, inheritance, investments, etc. Your paycheck is a resource. Your part-time job is a resource.

In the space below, write down each of your goals from the goal-setting exercise.

GOALS

Next, think of the resources you have available to you to help you achieve those goals.

RESOURCES

Where is your money?

We can't close out a discussion about getting started without discussing where you keep your money.

There are several options for storing your money:

1. **Anti- Establishment:** Your money stays with you and could burn up if your house does.
2. **For-Profit Bank:** Chase, Bank of America, Ally, Capital One, Regions, US Bank, etc.
3. **Credit Union**
4. **Prepaid Debit Card**

PayPal is not listed here because PayPal is not a bank though it offers similar functions.

When working with clients, I have found that having at least two different accounts with separate banks works best for creating boundaries between a savings and checking account. I'll explain this in a little more detail later.

If you are self-employed, you will need more accounts. While I don't go into detail regarding the types of accounts needed if you are a business owner, I highly suggest you read the book, *Profit First: Transform Your Business from a Cash-Eating Monster to a Money-Making Machine* by Mike Michalowicz. It helped me tremendously as I transitioned from managing my personal finances as a traditional employee to managing my finances as an entrepreneur.

In a 2015 survey conducted by the FDIC, 60 percent of households reported they banked traditionally. Among those respondents were people who banked at for-profit institutions and credit unions. Due to their relentless marketing and presence in communities, most people are familiar with banks, but less familiar with credit unions.

A credit union is a not-for-profit organization owned by all its members versus a for-profit bank owned by a small group of individuals.

The first official credit union was founded in Germany, in the 1880s, by a group of farmers who were turned away by traditional banks. Today, most credit unions are federally insured, full-service financial institutions offering products and services, such as personal (and business) checking and savings accounts, investment accounts, home and auto loans, credit building products, debt solutions, credit cards, and more.

Credit unions typically offer better interest rates than traditional banks because they reinvest extra funds generated back into the company, enabling them to provide lower rates to their members. The majority of credit unions offer free checking accounts, which have no maintenance fees, no minimum balance fees, and no transaction fees.

Pre-paid cards are increasing in popularity as they become easier to put money onto and use. They can be a valuable asset for someone seeking to control their spending, because most cards don't allow you to spend over the balance in your account. Pre-paid cards, however, have a reputation for being predatory, making it imperative to monitor the fees you are being charged for using them.

Now that you have assessed where you are, let's explore the different components of a core financial foundation.

Chapter 2

Savings Strategies and Solutions

Savings is money from your disposable income not spent on consumer goods. It is put aside—without any intention of spending it—for a specific purpose or future need. Your savings, along with your budget, are the most important components of your financial picture, which is why we'll start the foundation conversation by exploring them.

Savings is not only important because it allows you to buy things, but also because it can help prevent you from going into debt in the event of an unexpected expense. When you have enough money in savings, you don't have to rely on credit cards (which create debt) and you don't have to do things that compromise your power. Knowing you have money at your disposal helps you sleep easier. The truth is, you don't "credit" your way to financial freedom. You save and invest your way to it.

If you are struggling with the decision to pay your debt versus build your savings, I suggest you consider prioritizing your savings (unless you are facing legal action or eviction). A lack of savings will contribute to more debt, but a lack of debt won't contribute to your savings.

How much you save largely depends on your goals and current financial obligations including those individuals who depend on you. If you have dependents, you need to save more because your finances aren't just covering you.

Your reserves need to be sufficient to cover your household bills while making sure the individuals depending on you have their necessities.

The more you're responsible for, the more you need to save.

How much should you save?

A common rule of thumb is to save six months of your household expenses. So, if your monthly overhead is $3,000, you should have at least $18,000 set aside in your savings account.

The average job seeker searches for a job for three to six months. In the event of short or long-term disabilities, unexpected death, or other external factors, you would require even more set aside in savings to ensure you're able to cover the minimum expenses.

If you aren't aware of your monthly household expenses, you can tally it in the budgeting section of this book.

Other schools of thought suggest a target amount of $10,000, which would definitely cover the overhead of a typical family for at least two to four months.

If you're reading this and thinking to yourself, GIRL, I'm just trying to save something: $1,000, $100, $10...something, I get it. If you haven't saved anything, or if you are rebuilding your savings, these amounts can feel overwhelming. It is completely understandable. And with the following tips, strategies, and dedication on your part, you can transform your savings account from a desert to a reservoir.

Make it a goal to save at least 10 percent of your income as regularly and as often as possible.

If you've never saved a substantial amount of money before...

I'll preface this by saying, substantial is relative and will likely depend on your income and resources.

Prove to yourself you can save. Strive to set a personal best record, which will be different for everyone. Most of us are partial to whole, neat numbers, so consider starting with increments relative to your available income. For example, if you're financially stretched, try reaching for $100, then $250, then $500, $750, $1,000, and so on.

If you've saved before...

Aim to match your personal best. This should only include amounts you have saved from your income. This does not include savings accumulated from bonuses, tax returns, inheritances, or other lump sum amounts you have set aside for savings. While money saved from windfalls spends just like money saved from your income, it might not happen as frequently. And the mission is to create savings goals that feel attainable and inspire you to keep going.

Once you match your personal best, aim to save 25 percent more. Then, calculate the desired savings amount by multiplying by 0.25.

For example:
If your personal best is $1,600, this is how it would look:

$1,600 x 0.25= $400. Now add $400 (the 25% increase) to $1,600 (your previous personal best) and you'd get $2,000.

Now, your new savings goal would be $2,000.

From there, you would strive to save your monthly overhead, and then begin accumulating several months' worth of savings until you have reached six months saved.

If you don't have any outstanding debt or other financial obligations and have already started investing, by all means, continue to save. If you have debt which needs to be eliminated (other than student loan debt), pause right here, and focus on other areas of your financial picture.

Depending on where you are in your journey, here are suggested savings benchmarks.

For The Traditionally Employed:

- One day's salary (weekly salary divided by how many days a week you work)
- One week's salary
- Two weeks' salary
- One-month's salary
- Three months' salary
- Six months' salary
- Nine months' salary
- One year's salary

For The Self-Employed Or Those With Inconsistent Income:

- Half of your monthly overhead
- One month of your monthly overhead
- Three months of your monthly overhead
- Six months of your monthly overhead
- One year of your monthly overhead

For those of you reading this and thinking to yourself, Save what with what? because you're living paycheck to paycheck and feeling like you barely have enough to cover your necessities (let alone save), you'll have to get a little more creative and be more flexible.

The first thing you want to consider is reducing your expenses so that you have breathing room in your budget.

- Is it time to get a roommate or move to a less expensive living option?

- Can you reduce your utility costs or subscriptions by taking advantage of promotions, downgrading your package, or eliminating the expense altogether?

- Do you really need the triple play package?

- Do you need to start doing some or all of your own cosmetic services (e.g., manicures, pedicures, etc.), or do you need to have a hair style you can maintain without numerous visits to the salon?

We will explore more expense-cutting options during the budgeting section, but remember, you have options. You always have options. A friend of mine (and her husband) realized they wouldn't be able to save for a down payment for their home while they were renting. Their solution was to move into my friend's father's house with their two kids. Her father has a decent-sized house, but it wasn't a mansion by any means. Sixteen months later, my friend and her family moved into their brand-new home, built from the ground up.

Some people say they can't do roommates in their space, but if my friend could move her entire family into her father's house as an option, I encourage you to think beyond short-term comfort so you can flourish long term.

What to look for in a savings account

As mentioned previously, you should put your saved funds into an "inconvenient" savings account. I'm not talking offshore inconvenient, but at a financial institution apart from your primary institution(s). Don't carry the debit card for the savings account. This will help protect you from yourself by putting an extra step between you and your money. This will also encourage you to withdraw the money you're saving for a need, not a want.

Remember, your emergency fund is not for emergency fun.

Needs vary from person to person. A need is a necessity, without which you would not have the minimum needed to live life comfortably. The more exemptions you make for needs, the less likely you are to reach your stated goals. So, while the sample sale splurges you dipped into your savings for may seem minimal and totally worth it, the act of violating your own boundaries chips away at the foundation of discipline you are creating.

When considering the savings accounts best for you, there are a few things you want to take into consideration.

Interest Rate

While this will be nominal, it's still something. The average savings account interest rate typically hovers around 0.06 percent depending on the economy. It is nice to have your savings work for you, but unless you have a significant amount saved, you're not exactly going to get rich off the interest generated from your savings account.

Fees

Fees are the costly, yet quiet vandal. You don't want to have your hard-earned money eaten up by fees. (This wisdom also applies to checking and savings accounts.) There are banking options that don't charge you fees. If you're unsure whether or not your current bank charges fees, check your statement. If you aren't able to determine the answer, contact the bank to inquire whether or not they charge fees. If your savings is currently in an account which charges fees, ask the bank if they have another option without fees or consider the necessary actions you can take to avoid being charged fees. Some banks will waive fees if you have automatic deposits or maintain a certain account balance.

Convenience

You want the bank to be inconvenient for quick withdrawals, but not too inconvenient. Since most banking functions are conducted electronically, you'll want a bank with the technology available for you to bank online so you can check your balances and transfer money in case of an emergency. In general, transfers take 2-4 business days which is sufficient time to deal with most emergencies. If a financial institution takes more time to transfer, you might want to consider your options.

Customer Service

If the customer service experience is important to you, then you'll want to take this into consideration as well. Don't only consider the quality of service received, but also the service options available. Financial institutions that operate online often provide virtual customer support. If you prefer to speak to someone face to face occasionally or frequently, then a brick-and-mortar option located within driving distance would likely be your best option.

Non-Traditional Savings Options

In certain communities, there are communal savings funds also known as sou sou. A sou sou (also spelled sou, su-su or susu) is an informal savings club, where a group of people get together and contribute an equal amount of money into a shared fund at agreed-upon time intervals (e.g., weekly, bi-weekly, monthly). The pooled money, or pot, is paid to one member of the club on a previously agreed-upon schedule, which is typically weekly or monthly. The pot makes its way around the group until all members have received their share of what they've deposited.

Sou sous have been used for years, particularly in communities where banking options weren't widely available to members of the community. Sou sous shouldn't replace a traditional savings account. They could, however, supplement your savings strategy or be used to jumpstart your account. They are not FDIC insured, and you cannot easily withdraw from them (at will or out of schedule). Sou sous do not pay interest, and you want to make sure the person in charge of managing and distributing the money is ethical.

Creative Ways to Save

We've spoken about the fundamentals of savings, but let's talk about creative ways to save in your everyday life that you might not have considered. A word of warning, most financial advice and strategies are cut and dry. Meaning, you can only get so creative about saving money. There comes a point where you have to stop looking for creativity and start looking for ways to take action.

One of the easiest ways to save is to use a lump sum of money—or a bonus—to make significant progress toward your savings goal.

Savings Strategies and Solutions

Here are a few ideas you might not have considered:

- Reduce your electricity bill by lowering your hot water heater's temperature.

- Adjust your tax withholding.

- Call your providers to find out if you're getting the best price for your usage.

- Dry your clothing on a line outside or a clotheshorse indoors.

- Plant a garden and grow some of your own herbs and vegetables to reduce your grocery bill.

- Drink water, not soda.

- Cancel the gym membership and workout at home using YouTube videos or run in your neighborhood.

- Compare your rental and auto insurance premiums annually to make sure you're getting the best rate.

- Gift your skills and time instead of spending money.

- Make your coffee at home instead of regularly visiting costly coffee shops. (Discount stores have great flavors and options.)

- Create and use a price book. Record prices of items you use regularly to ensure you are always getting the best deal.

- Shop your closet or borrow from a friend instead of buying new items.

- Do a clothing swap with friends instead of shopping for new clothes.

- Use your points on your credit cards.

- Unsubscribe to e-mails from stores to avoid temptation!

- Cut back on drinking alcohol while dining out.
- Take advantage of cashback programs.

To Automate or Not to Automate

Automating your savings deposits directly from your account or paycheck is by far one of the easiest ways to accumulate savings and eliminate the dependency on your memory when it comes to saving.

Automating your savings could include one of the following:

1. Depositing a portion of your paycheck directly into your savings account.
2. Scheduling automatic transfers to your savings account on specific days, ideally payday or the next business day following your payday.

Most financial institutions allow you to set up a regularly recurring transfer of funds from your main account to a savings account. Just make sure they do not charge a fee for this service.

Keep in mind, you can adjust your transfers or deposits at any time should life or circumstances change.

Automating savings isn't for everyone. I happen to love manual savings because of the sense of accomplishment

I feel moving the money to where I know it will work for me. I am also an entrepreneur and my income amounts vary. One of the drawbacks to automating savings is the possibility of overdraft fees. For example, if an emergency arises and you need more of your money, the bank might not be able to cancel the transfer in time, which could lead to overdraft fees or a delay in the access of funds.

Individual Development Accounts

Before we close the conversation on savings, I want to share a resource that is often overlooked and underutilized: Individual Development Accounts, often referred to as IDAs.

IDAs enable low-income American families to save. Additionally, they promote savings among underserved populations by matching the savings amount of what clients deposit. While some of these programs have specific savings outcome objectives to help account holders buy their first home, begin investing, pay for post-secondary education, or start a small business, they are also created to encourage savings.

To find an IDA program serving your local community, look up the following term "IDA [enter your state or county]". Most often, these programs will be offered by nonprofits that partner with banking institutions. Some may have income maximums and family size requirements you must meet in order to be eligible.

In conclusion, savings is essential, not optional.

If you've struggled with saving in the past, the goal isn't to save big. The goal is to create a habit of putting money aside even if it's a smaller amount. It's about creating a habit of savings and not spending it. The habit is combined with the discipline that creates a savings account.

If you've saved in the past, you've done it before and can successfully do it again.

Chapter 3

Getting a Handle on Debt

The Debt Journey

I grew up in North Carolina, in a middle-class family or as my mom would say, "Upper middle-class community," comprised primarily of working class people of color, who were able to afford a nice home, car, etc. Even so, I was around a lot of debt creation.

Human beings are pack animals and have an innate desire to belong. For many, the desire to belong leads to debt. This phenomena is often referred to as "Keeping up with the Joneses." This English-language phrase refers to individuals who live beyond their means in order to achieve or maintain social status. Keeping up with the Joneses and debt have become a way of life in America. According to CNBC, in 2015, 8 out of 10 Americans had some form of debt.

One of the challenges we face as consumers is wading through the barrage of aggressive and subliminal marketing messages encouraging us to spend against our better judgment. Advertising executives and behavioral scientists dedicate their days to finding ways to convince us to spend.

Common marketing tactics include:

1. Appealing to our desire to belong

2. Appealing to our need for reward

3. Strategic positioning of products in stores and on social media

4. Creating urgency and forcing us to act on impulse and not logic

These marketing tactics affect our decision-making ability. Before we know it, we find ourselves in debt and scampering to regain our financial footing. Anyone who has accumulated debt can tell you it is one of the easiest things to do. You harmlessly swipe a card in exchange for goods and/or services, and the result is often an unexpected and intimidating credit card balance.

Debt can be stressful, often causing feelings of hopelessness. The average American family has debt. It has become a way of life. As marketing companies and capitalism fuel the desire to buy more things, they don't address the emotions that accompany buying too many things or accumulating debt you can't afford. Debt is a leading cause of suicide; which is often the result of the helplessness, loneliness, and shame individuals feels because of their debt.

There is life outside of debt and you have options.

In this chapter, we will discuss your options and the ways you can begin to put a dent in your debt. If you aren't able to immediately put a dent in your debt and need to come back to this section, that is okay. If you need to tread water and come up for air before organizing and attacking your debt, that is okay, too. Just remember you are not alone. Many have accumulated debt and are climbing their way out of it successfully, just as you can and will.

If you are feeling hopeless, here are a few things to remember:

You can't be arrested just because you owe money on consumer debt (we will discuss this later), unless debt collectors sue you and win a judgment against you. In some states, debtors can be arrested if the court ordered them to pay the debt holder and they did not. The arrest would be for defying the court though, not for owing the money.

It is illegal for debt collectors to threaten you with arrest.

You have rights when it comes to how companies collect debt from you, and they can lose their licensing and right to collect from others for violating these laws.

- It's illegal for a debt collector to come to your workplace to collect payment.

- Debt collectors cannot call you at work if you request that they do not call you at work.

- Debt collectors cannot harass you with repeated calls, threats of violence, published information about you, and/or abusive or obscene language in their attempts to collect from you.

- Debt collectors cannot call you before 8 a.m. and after 9 p.m.

It is illegal for your employer to fire you solely because you have debt (but if you allow the debt to affect your performance and workplace integrity, it could create fertile grounds for termination).

Bankruptcy is an option, and people have successfully recovered from bankruptcy (six words: 45th President of the United States).

You have rights and protections when it comes to debt. No individual should feel that the amount of debt owed is more valuable than their life and what they mean to those who love them. Money isn't everything. It gives you options, but it isn't everything. In the moments you feel hopeless about debt, it is important to remember all that you are to the people who love you.

If you are still feeling suicidal about your debt, please contact the National Suicide Prevention Lifeline at 1-800-273-8255. They are available 24 hours a day.

Now, let's discuss different types of debt: secured and unsecured.

Secured debt is debt backed or secured by collateral to reduce the risk associated with lending (e.g., a mortgage). If the borrower doesn't pay, the bank has an asset they can take ownership of and minimize their losses.

Unsecured debt is a loan not backed by an asset (e.g., a home, a vehicle). Unsecured debt can be accumulated from credit cards, medical bills, utility bills, and other types of loans or credit extended without a collateral requirement.

The most common category of unsecured debt is consumer debt (e.g. credit card debt, medical debt, student loan debt).

While our goal is to live a debt-minimal life, it is important to discuss the concept of "good" debt. Some argue for it; some argue against it. Risks are associated with any debt, whether it is considered good or bad. The purpose of this explanation isn't to make you feel good or bad about the forms of debt you have. The purpose is to help you think about future debt before you acquire it.

"Good debt" is defined as any debt that will help you generate future or current income and is incurred as a means of creating wealth. Even if you don't see yourself living a debt-free lifestyle, make it a goal to at least eliminate bad debt and minimize emergency debt (medical debt or debt acquired for things you may need, but don't have enough in savings or investments to purchase in cash).

Examples of good debt are as follows:

- Real Estate or Mortgage Loans
- Small Business Loans
- Well-thought-out Educational Loans

"Bad debt" is any debt obtained for the consumption of depreciating items. This type of debt does not generate additional income and loses value over time. Bad debts are typically incurred on items you can't afford or don't need. More often, the amounts you pay in interest, penalties, and late payment fees are higher than the services or products received.

Examples of bad debt are as follows:

- Store Cards for Consumable Purchases (e.g., furniture, clothing, groceries, gasoline, travel, jewelry)
- Credit Cards

- Borrowing from a 401k
- Payday Loans

Avoid payday loan debt and rent-to-own debt. If you already have it, prioritize eliminating those debts as soon as possible. If you don't have them, avoid them at all costs.

Payday loans and rent-to-own debt are the crabs of the debt barrel and are often predatory. They exploit the financial conditions of borrowers who feel like they don't have options. Interest rates from these types of debt are often unreasonable and difficult for financially-challenged individuals to pay back. One extreme example of these problematic loans is a "car title loan". With this type of loan the lender requires that the borrower put down a vehicle title as collateral to secure the loan. If the loan goes unpaid for a specific time frame the lender will take possession of the borrowers vehicle to satisfy the loan even if the value of the vehicle exceeds the loan amount, leaving the borrower with a car payment but no car if they had a loan on the vehicle.

When it comes to debt, most of us know we have it, but we don't necessarily know how much we have. Not knowing often contributes to feeling overwhelmed. I'm not saying writing out your debts will automatically make you feel better about your debt, but it does help you put things into perspective.

Now, we've covered the debt basics. Next, I want you to list your debts to get a clear understanding of how much debt you have using the following Debt Overview table which you can find in the workbook.

Once you have listed your debts, determine the best debt-elimination strategy for you.

I understand that if I'm discussing debt I should discuss student loans. I cover student loans in detail in Chapter 6.

So let's discuss debt elimination. Here are three effective strategies you can use to eliminate debt:

1. Snowball Repayment Method

Have you ever built a snowman? You start with a small ball and continue to add snow until the ball becomes bigger and bigger. Eventually, it becomes so big that you just roll the ball around collecting more snow.

Start small and build up to something awesome.

That is how the debt snowball repayment method works; you start with small debt payments, achieving small wins along the way, and build momentum over time. As you pay off smaller debts, you reallocate the money to the next larger debt and continue this practice until all debt is paid.

Pros

- Starting with the smallest payments can provide quick wins and a sense of accomplishment.

- As you eliminate your smaller balances, you can free up extra funds to focus on the next balance.

Cons

- It may take longer to pay off your debt.

- You could pay more in interest over time.

2. Debt Avalanche Method

With this method, you arrange your debts by interest rate rather than dollar amount and pay the debts with the highest interest rate first.

Picture an avalanche. It starts at the top of the mountain and cascades downward until it reaches the bottom. Using the debt avalanche method, you pay down the highest interest rate loan first, while paying the minimum balance on the rest of your loans. Once the debt with the highest rate is paid off, you move on to the next highest interest debt, and so on, until all of the debt is paid off.

For example, if you have debt at 15.9 percent, 9.8 percent, and zero percent, you would work on eliminating your 15.9 percent interest rate debt first, regardless of the balance. Once you have paid it off, you would then focus on the 9.8 percent debt, then the zero percent debt.

Pros

- You spend less money in the long run because of the savings on interest.

Cons

- It can be hard to remain motivated.
- It may feel like it takes forever to pay off the high-interest debt if the balance is large.

3. The All-In Method

Under this method, you make the minimum payments on all of your debts except one "focus" debt. This is a debt of your choosing.

Hone in on this single debt and send every dollar you can towards the debt until it's gone, while making the minimum payments on the other debts.

Pros

- It's flexible and allows you to target the debt that bothers you most.
- You may spend less money in the long run, if you select a debt with higher interest.

Cons

- It may feel like it takes forever to pay off the debt, if you select a large balance debt with a higher interest rate.
- It may take longer to pay off your debt.
- You could pay more in interest over time.

If you're a numbers person who takes pleasure in the details, you can do a comparison of the costs over the life of the debt for each of the repayment strategies.

If you aren't a numbers person and details paralyze you, don't obsess over the lifetime costs of the methods. Just get started with eliminating your debt.

Should you consider bankruptcy?

If you don't have enough to pay your debts at this time, you have four options:

- Move things around so you can pay your debt.
- Acquire more work so you can pay off your debt.
- Put off paying your debt until you have the means.
- File bankruptcy.

While bankruptcy isn't always the most desirable outcome, in some instances, it makes sense for an individual who is deeply in debt to file, start over, and vow to avoid the financial mistakes of their past.

If you think bankruptcy might be the best option for you, I encourage you to reach out to a bankruptcy attorney. Do not choose the first bankruptcy attorney, but make sure you speak to at least three before you make a decision. All attorneys aren't created equal.

If you have accumulated debt, chances are you have also been approached by collection companies to collect on debts you owe. It's important not to avoid the collection companies.

Get the information in writing. According to the Debt Collection Act, within five days of contacting you, a collector must send you a written notice telling you the amount of money you owe, the name of the creditor, and what action to take if you believe you don't owe the money.

Do not engage in further conversations or negotiations with a debt collector, instead ask him or her to send you the information in writing, and then move forward.

Debt Collectors Can:

1. Ask You to Pay on a Debt Past the Statute of Limitations

Unsecured debts have a statute of limitations, meaning there's an age limit to the debt and a limit to the amount of time a creditor can ask the court to force you to pay for a debt. For most debts, it is seven years; however, each state might have their own statute of limitation laws. You are responsible for tracking the statute of limitations for your debt. Once the debt reaches its expiration date, collection companies can no longer sue you for it. The debt must be removed from your credit report, but you still owe the debt. It doesn't just disappear. Debt collectors can still seek payment for it, they just can't sue you for it.

2. Ask You to Sell Your Debt

Collection companies are in the business of buying old debts and profiting from them. They will also re-sell your debt, or a portion of it if they feel their collection efforts will be in vain. Just because one debt collector stops contacting you about a debt doesn't mean it's gone. More than likely, it means they are seeking a new buyer for the debt. Re-selling debts are a common practice in the collection business, which highlights the importance of getting all agreements and payments in writing in case you need to provide receipts of your payments.

3. Negotiate Your Debt

Because debt collection companies often purchase the debt for significantly less than it's worth, the debtor gains wiggle room to negotiate with collectors who will often settle the debt for less than the amount owed. If you determine the debt is legitimately yours, contact the company to find out if they'd be willing to accept half the amount or settle for less than the amount owed.

What to do if you don't have enough to pay your debts.

From that point, it's important to remember that while you may feel the debt needs to be eliminated immediately, consider the financial implications of eliminating the debt. Weigh the advantages and disadvantages of paying the debt right now versus focusing on establishing financial security, and then refocusing on debt elimination.

If none of these options are available to you, then you need to decide which debts to pay off first with your limited funds.

The debt that poses the most impact to your family's quality of life should be tackled first (e.g., past due rent, an auto title loan—which puts you at risk of losing your vehicle, a personal loan—which if left unpaid, could ruin a relationship).

In order to find money to pay your debt if you're financially strained, you will have to either make room in your existing budget, find ways to bring in more money, or do both.

What if you default on your student loans?

If you pay your student loans monthly, your loan is considered to be in default if you haven't made any payments on it for 270 days (nine months) or haven't made arrangements with your servicer. You want to avoid this by any means necessary and communicate with your lenders if you are not able to pay your loans. Servicers offer forbearance, deferment, and retroactive versions of these options, which could save you money as well as a credit score dip.

If those options won't work and your loan is in default, there are three options for getting your federal loan out of default:

1. Contact Your Loan Servicer
Request your loan be removed from default status.

2. Loan Repayment
Pay your loan in full. Most of us don't have that option available to us, so you should try to negotiate a monthly repayment plan.

3. Loan Rehabilitation:
- Direct Loan Borrowers – You must make at least nine full payments of the agreed amount, within 20 days of their monthly due dates, over a 10-month period to the US DOE. Wage and tax garnishments will not be

counted toward your nine qualifying payments. Once you have made the nine payments, your loan(s) will be returned to loan servicing.

- FFEL Loan Borrowers – The same applies; however, once you have made nine payments, an eligible institution may purchase your loans.

- Perkins Loan Borrowers – You must make at least nine on-time monthly payments. Once you have made the required payments, your loan(s) will continue to be serviced by the Department of Education until the balance owed is paid in full.

Once your loans have been rehabilitated, your monthly payments will probably increase, and collection costs may be added to your principal balance. Delinquent payments reported before your loan defaulted will be removed from your credit report.

Private loans might not have the following rehabilitation options available, and despite attempts to negotiate, they still might send your student loan to collections. These loans are handled differently because you're dealing with a financial institution, not the government. If you are facing legal action from a private loan servicer, you should contact a student loan specialist or a student loan attorney who can advocate on your behalf and explore the options available to you.

It's important to do your research with anyone offering financial assistance, but especially companies promising to "fix" your student loans. Ask for references, and check out what people are saying about them online and in the comments sections of their social media posts and websites. There are a lot of companies profiting from people's desperation without delivering the promised results.

Making More Money to Pay off Your Debt

While your financial situation is largely attributed to your spending habits, some people actually have an income issue. In order to make more money, you have a couple options:

- Ask for a raise at your current job.
- Get a side job aka a side hustle to bring in additional income.

Side hustles—one of the untold secrets of households — help break the constraints of financial insecurity. In 1989, my parents stocked shelves at the military supermarket to earn side income. In 2018, individuals are driving on weekends, operating online stores, renting spare rooms in their houses, and taking advantage of technology to generate additional income.

The shared economy not only changed the way we do and experience business, but it also changed the way we bring in revenue. Today, earning additional money is easier than ever.

A side hustle is simply a way to make extra money outside of your day job. If it isn't generating income, it is a hobby.

The type of side hustle you select depends on your availability. In order for a side hustle to become a viable income stream, you need to treat it BETTER than you treat your primary source of income. If you are using side income to get you out of debt or to build a savings account, be sure to do the following:

- Draft a plan for how you will apply the income earned.

- Create a separate account for your money generated from the income, so it isn't mixed into your primary income or spent on things that don't contribute to your financial freedom.

When it comes to making more money, you have a few more options that might help with an initial pinch. You can sell goods, get paid for your services, and earn money for your expertise to bring in additional money.

These options don't require you to ask your employer for a raise, although you should do that too (as a way to advocate for what you believe you deserve).

Eliminating Expenses

I don't believe in deprivation as a financial freedom strategy, but I do believe there will be times when you have to make initial or short-term sacrifices in order to become more comfortable financially in the long term. Audit your life for things you can live without. Identify what's most important to your life and what will affect your livelihood the most if you don't do it.

Then, ask yourself what the trade off is. You can cut out the daily Starbucks trip, but you can't replace it with something else, such as eating out. The goal isn't to go cold turkey and eliminate everything because you increase the likelihood of failure by taking away multiple items you really enjoy. Instead, attempt to eliminate at least one thing—ideally the most expensive item—and keep the others. As you become more comfortable doing without items you once felt you needed, consider cutting more out.

Paying off debt sounds easier than it actually is. Debt elimination can be difficult. It often evokes feelings of deprivation, a sentiment in contrast to the one felt when goods and/or services are purchased because the gratification of new purchases is forced to take a backseat. It may feel like deprivation or even punishment because the desire to acquire new items is never ending.

There is a strong possibility you will feel like you're missing out. You will feel it when you look at your friends and they're all out at brunch posting on social media and so forth. Your social life might change as a result of your commitment to your financial goals.

You may not feel as confident because instead of spending money on clothes, you'll be spending money to eliminate your debt. Michael McCallowitz also said in Profit First: Transform Your Business from a Cash-Eating Monster to a Money-Making Machine that, "You have to get more joy out of saving money than you get out of spending it." And as you're going through the transition of getting more joy in paying off your debt, keep reminding yourself that you're essentially buying your freedom and escaping the bondage of debt.

It's all worth it in the long run though.

While it's wonderful to have good credit, adequate savings and minimal debt will put you in a better position to financially and holistically succeed.

Debt and financial stress bleed into other areas of our lives. Just think how much more purposeful, clear, and focused our lives would be if we didn't have debt hanging over our heads.

Debt elimination is a critical step towards financial freedom. Elimination of debt is achievable.

Chapter 4

Budgeting

Budgeting, the "B" word everyone dreads. For many people, budgeting represents restriction, when in actuality, a budget represents a plan in which the cliché statement, "A failure to plan is a plan to fail" rings true. Creating a budget is the first step, but actually living by a budget is a completely different process.

I'm going to be completely honest here. I'm not perfect when it comes to abiding by a monthly budget, but I do live by a spending plan.

What's the difference between a budget and a spending plan?

A budget is based on forecasting how much you will spend in each area of your life in order to maximize your income. A spending plan is very similar, but allows for more flexibility. Both provide you with directives for how you spend your money. A budget is more of an outline of your income as opposed to your expenses, and it is followed by allocating your expenses accordingly.

When you're just getting started with analyzing your finances or assessing your overall situation, you should begin with a budget. As you gain control of your financial situation and have a better understanding of where you stand financially, you can consider adjusting your money management strategy from a budget to a spending plan.

Before we get into creating your actual budget, it's important to understand the types of expenses you incur each month. Here, they are broken into three categories: needs, obligations, and wants.

Needs

These are items or expenses you must have in order to live or survive. Shelter, utilities, food, clothing, and transportation are examples of needs. While some would dispute whether or not you actually need these items, these are the basic items the average human being needs to function effectively in today's society.

The bare minimum requirement for a need varies by personal preference and individual need. There is a wide range of options for shelter, utilities, food, clothing, and transportation. Sometimes, there is a difference between your individual tastes and preferences and what you can afford.

Obligations

These are financial responsibilities you must pay because you owe money or have been ordered to pay someone money. Debts are examples of obligations. Child support, alimony, and court-mandated judgments are examples of obligations.

Category	Percentage of Overall Spending
Housing	25-35%
Utilities	5-10%
Transportation	10-15%
Healthcare	5-10%
Food	5-15%
Investments/Savings	5-10%
Debt Payments	5-10%
Charitable Giving	5-15%
Entertainment/Recreation	5-9%
Miscellaneous Personal	2-7%

Wants

These are the things you can survive without in life. Recreational activities and entertainment are examples of wants. Certain items can exist in a gray area and can span the need and want category, such as a new car with expensive features. While a reliable car (to get to work) is a need, a vehicle outfitted with costly, additional features may be what you want.

The reason we make money is to (1) pay for things we need and (2) buy things we want. I'm not going to tell you not to want things. I think wants can be healthy and motivating; however, if you are financially stressed and determine your expenses for your needs exceed your spending on your wants, it is important to have a conversation with yourself about permanently (or temporarily) reducing your wants until you are back on track financially.

Please note that these are just guidelines and may vary based on family size, location, and other factors. You can use the Percentage of Overall Spending table above to assess your current expenses and how far they are from the suggested percentages.

Now that we've flushed out types of expenses, let's get into the grit work of creating your budget.

A budget is strongly suggested for individuals who are living above their means, experiencing difficulty covering monthly expenses. A budget is for individuals who tend to excessively spend income on non-needs, resulting in the inability to cover their needs and financial obligations.

One of the things I love about budgeting is it helps you take a snapshot of your income versus expenses. It also provides you with a really clear picture of whether or not you're living at, or above, your means.

There are a few different types of budgets to consider, and the type of budget you enlist should be based on your payment intervals as well as your personal preferences. The different types of budgets are as follows. Following the budget descriptions, you will find a template to get you started with creating your budget.

Traditional Budget

The traditional budget, also known as a monthly budget, is the most common budgeting format. On a chart, write out all of your income for the month. Then, below it, write out your expenses for the month, subtracting your income from expenses. This type of budget is popular because it works for a variety of payment intervals and household dynamics.

Weekly Budget

The weekly budget is based on your expenses for the week. While the monthly budget takes the entire month into account, the weekly budget looks at the week or weeks ahead. It works best for people who are paid weekly.

Often, a variety of budgeting methods are needed. The weekly budget may be implemented as a short-term (or special occasion) money management strategy, such as budgeting for a vacation or life event. This method may require you to combine short-term savings from week to week for a larger monthly expense, such as rent if weekly income is not enough to cover it.

Zero-Based Budgeting

This budgeting method, essentially, requires you to give every single dollar a specific job. Meaning, you plan to have "zero" money left over at the end of the month because you have diligently accounted for every way you could possibly use your money.

Now, this doesn't mean you have zero dollars in your bank account. It just means your income minus all your expenses equals zero. For example, if you earn $3,000 a month, you want everything you spend, save, donate, give, and/or invest to add up to $3,000. The purpose of zero-based budgeting is to know exactly where every one of your dollars is going.

Percentage-Based Budgeting

There are two type of percentage-based budgets. One is the 50/30/20 budget strategy, a slightly more relaxed take on budgeting as opposed to the line-item budgeting process employed in the previous examples.

This model allows for 50 percent of income to be spent on needs, while 20 percent is set aside for savings and financial goals, and the remaining 30 percent is reserved for wants and non-essential purchases, such a cosmetic services, clothing purchases, and activities like concerts, movies, and sporting events.

You can choose to list the individual line items for each of these categories, or you can choose not to, once you've broken your income down into each respective category.

Budgeting

If you choose to implement this budgeting strategy, I suggest you open separate accounts to make it easier to remain within intended percentage allocations. For example, the account you deposit checks into could serve as your needs account, while an account with another institution could serve as your wants account.

In the savings section, we discussed the advantages of establishing an inconvenient savings account for your savings. This method can be challenging for individuals who have expenses that exceed 50 percent of their income; however, it is a great budget for someone who is just starting out and building their lifestyle while keeping their budget in mind as they add on new expenses.

During the budgeting activity, we will check your spending to assess how much of your income you are spending on each of the categories. You can use the budget provided in the Money Manual workbook or complete this activity on a ssheet of paper.

Even if you have created a budget before I suggest you create another budget as your income and expenses might have changed since the last time you created a budget. Additionally, the following activity may resonate with you more than your previous attempts in the past.

Step 1: Look at your previous month's spending

This strategy will be easy for people who are currently living within their means and lifestyle. It could be slightly more difficult for people just starting out, such as recent graduates or people working to establish financial freedom for the first time.

The easiest way to begin is to print out a summary of your spending for the last 30 days, or pull up a PDF of last month's bank statement.

If you have not banked electronically in this past, this step will be challenging for you, but do your best.

In the section below, you can find a list of common spending categories.

Savings
This category includes all your savings goals, but is not limited to emergencies, your education, your children's education, retirement, your "quit your job fund," holiday purchases, travel, back-to-school shopping, etc.

Debt Payments
Credit cards, student loans, business loans, installment loans, payday loans, car title loan payments as well as other loan payments

Housing
Rent, mortgage, insurance, property taxes, repairs, community dues

Utilities
Electricity, gas, water, sewage, phone, television, internet service, cell phone

Household Supplies and Home Improvement
Cleaning services, lawn services, cleaning supplies, furniture and décor, kitchen appliances, furniture, other equipment

Groceries
Food and beverages you bring into the home to prepare, including baby food and formula

Eating Out (meals & beverages)
Any meal or beverage purchased outside of the home

Pets
Food, healthcare costs, and other costs associated with caring for your pets

Transportation
Gas, car payment, insurance payment, repairs, public transportation, tickets, and fines

Health Care
Co-payments, medication, eye care, dental care, health care premiums, Personal Care Haircuts, Hygiene Items, Dry Cleaning

Childcare and School Costs
Diapers, filed trips, school-related supplies, materials, expenses, and fees, as well as other activity fees

Clothing
New clothing, laundry and cleaning, alterations

Business
Any expenses associated with the running of a business (e.g. software, membership dues, staff, marketing materials, etc).

Entertainment
Movies, concerts, sporting events, sports entertainment equipment/fees, lottery tickets, memberships, alcohol, books/CDs, subscriptions

Court-ordered obligations
Child support, alimony, restitution, etc.

Tithes, Gifts, Donations
Donations to religious organizations or other charities, gifts, expenses

Miscellaneous

Any expense that doesn't fall into the categories listed above

Complete your budget in your companion Money Manual Workbook.

DAILY EXPENSE TRACKER

DATE	DESCRIPTION	CATEGORY	AMOUNT	CASH CREDIT OR DEBIT	NEED/WANT

Once you add up all your items you have identified as needs, you can determine how much your life costs you.

List it here:

My life costs: _____

Now, look at your number. Ask yourself, is this number in line with what I expected my life to cost? Is it more? Less? This step is helpful because, often times, we load on expenses without having an understanding of how it impacts our total monthly budget.

Budgeting

Have another look at your spending tracker but this time, lets trim the excess. Are there items that you spent money on that can be completely eliminated or reduced?

Put a line through any expenses that could be eliminated

Lastly, identify any areas that allow flexibility, such as reducing the frequency of winter-time pedicures by maintaining your own pedicures with at-home pedicure tools? In the to-do list below, write out what you need to do to eliminate/ reduce your expenses.

For example:

- Contact cable company and cancel cable.
- Cancel upcoming nail appointment.

TO DO

TRACK PROGRESS

Now that you have listed your spending, let's create a typical line-item budget.

List all sources of income at the top. This includes job earnings, child support, alimony, inheritance, social security benefits, unemployment income, and any income you receive regularly.

Entrepreneurs!
If some, or all, of your income comes from your business, this will be slightly more challenging since your income can vary, so I suggest you take an average of your income.

Utilize your invoice management software, such as Intuit QuickBooks, to determine your income for the past three months, before expenses, and take an average of the three:

[(Month 1 + Month 2 + Month 3)/ 3].

If you do not use income management software, look at your bank account statements and/or electronic payment summaries for the past three months and identify the "check deposited" or "money deposited" amounts. Just make sure you don't duplicate any deposit amounts, which could artificially inflate your numbers.

Using the template in the workbook, fill in the "needs" categories based on what your needs cost each month.

For your "wants," fill in the categories based on the eliminations and reductions you made based on last month's spending.

Voila! You have yourself a budget!

As a finance professional, I can't talk about budgeting without discussing one of the most popular budgeting alternatives for non-budgeters or people who need a little more support in this area. It is known as the cash envelope budgeting system.

You may be familiar with the older version of a cash budgeting system that requires you to take your entire paycheck out and pay bills cash but let's be honest. Paying bills with cash can be a huge headache. Whether it be locating checks and hoping your checks are cashed in a reasonable time, securing money orders, or paying bills at a payment center (which often carries fees), paying bills with cash can be challenging. (Note: Please don't mail cash. Please don't.) So with that said, this isn't a true cash envelope budgeting system because it allows you to still pay certain bills online while paying cash for other budget categories. It's a New Age cash envelope budgeting system.

Here's how it works:
1. Determine Your Categories

Items you pay cash for should be given an envelope. These are items you can physically walk into a store to buy. You can opt to use a cash-based budgeting system for specific categories, such as entertainment, groceries, and/or dining out (especially if these are categories in which you frequently find yourself overspending).

Once you determine your categories, make a list of each cash category with exactly how much cash is going into the category each month.

2. Withdraw the Cash and Store It

Add all the categories together. This is the total amount of cash you will be withdrawing from your bank account each month.

You need a safe place to keep your cash envelopes, including one envelope for each category.

Create an envelope for each category. You can order specialized cash envelopes on Etsy or Amazon, or you can buy regular envelopes from the local discount store or office supplies store and label them based on how you intend to use the cash inside (i.e., groceries, school supplies, clothes, entertainment, etc.).
Pull the cash out the day you get paid, ideally before you start making purchases.

How much you take out and budget for will depend on how often you get paid. If you get paid once a month then you will be taking the entire amount of monthly cash out on that day.

If you get paid bi-weekly or on two specific days each month, you will divide your total monthly cash amount by two. This new number is the amount of money you need to take out of your bank account each payday.

If your payment dates are sporadic, set your own spending period based on the amount received and your next pay period. For example, you might want to budget for a week or an entire month, maybe even an entire quarter.

Separate your cash and allocate it to its respective envelope.

For example, if you plan to spend $150 on entertainment for the month, put $150 in the entertainment envelope and follow suit for each category.

3. Spend

You don't have to take all of your envelopes out with you all the time. Chances are if you're headed to the grocery store, you're not headed to the movies or another place of entertainment. But sometimes, your spending events will overlap, and you'll want to have multiple categories of cash with you.

After you spend, return the remainder to the envelope after counting how much money you have left. Depending on the envelope used, you can write the new amount for the month on the envelope to make it easier to determine what you have left/available for the month.

Once the cash is gone, it's gone! You've bottomed out on that budget item for the spending period.

Whether or not you want to spend the money for each category in the given month is up to you. As I frequently state, you don't have to spend every last dime you have.

If you have money left over at the end of your spending period, simply roll it over to the next month or qualifying event.

And that's it!

But What About Other Online Purchases?

The disadvantage of the envelope budgeting system is you might lose out on rewards received from making digital purchases or payments.

This budgeting system doesn't account for online expenses—which are often more cost effective—like purchasing supplies from Amazon or clothes from online retailers.

You can load your allocated spending amount for these categories onto a card from a separate online checking account. I have a card that I load my Christmas spending money onto, and it is separate from my checking accounts. Once the money is gone on this particular card, it's gone. This transaction is easier for online purchasing, rather than pulling cash out and loading it onto the card, you can transfer the cash over. In the resources section of this book, you will find the names of banks and companies that offer no fee and free checking. These banks and companies would work well for this purpose.

Make sure your cash is well organized. It is the key to running a successful cash envelope system. If your cash gets all mixed together, you'll likely get overwhelmed and abandon the system.

Remember, just because it doesn't work one month doesn't mean it won't work the next month.

Commitment over perfection is key.

While I'm not advocating spending unnecessarily, there are wallets specifically designed for the envelope budgeting system available for purchase online, making it easy for you to succeed at this budgeting method.

Identifying Budget Busting Spending Triggers

Budget busters happen. One of the most common budget busters is a spending trigger. Spending triggers are physical and emotional events that cause us to spend money. They can happen to the best of us.

If you've ever bought something you didn't intend to or overspent on an item purchase, it is likely a spending trigger of some sort prompted this purchase. Identifying what prompts you to spend is an important step in getting your spending under control and understanding the triggers which contributed to your temporary lapse in judgment.

Triggers differ from person to person. To help you get an idea of the types of triggers that may influence your decisions, let's take a look at a few examples below:

- Stress
- Grief
- Boredom
- Anger
- Happiness
- Lack of Rest
- Hunger
- Sickness

- Job Loss
- Vacations
- Celebrations (Births, Graduations, Reunions)
- Discounts

To understand your own spending triggers, self-reflection and expense tracking are necessary. Consider the last thing you purchased today. Was that item an impulse purchase or planned for expense? Spending triggers for necessities are quite different from those impulse buys.

Take note of this spending and reflect on the emotion or event that influenced your decision.

I want you to track your expenses for the next five days along with notes of how you were feeling the day of the purchase. Also, make note of any events that took place the day of the purchase. (Doing this will help you identify whether or not your spending is triggered by some of the events and/or emotions listed.) Once you know your triggers, come up with a plan to handle things differently.

Here are a few examples:

- Prep your meals ahead of time and always carry a snack when you go out. (This will hopefully defeat hunger and impulsive fast-food buys.)
- Try exercising when you're stressed, angry, or bored instead of shopping.
- Create (and use) a gift budget to handle unexpected life celebrations.

What are a few other things you can do to address your spending triggers?

List your triggers below. Beside them, list what you can do the next time the trigger arises.

I find myself spending money that I do not plan to spend when I...   *Instead of spending money, when I feel this way, I can...*

_____   _____

_____   _____

_____   _____

_____   _____

_____   _____

_____   _____

_____   _____

Budgeting When There Isn't Enough

Even when you cut spending, you may still find yourself short on cash.

But when you're trying to decide which of your obligations to pay first and bill collectors are calling, it often seems easiest to pay the "squeakiest wheel" or the account that's demanding the most attention.

You are responsible for paying all of your obligations on time. But when you've cut out everything that is not a "need" and truly do not have enough money to cover your obligations and living expenses, you may have to make a short-term plan to get through the month. And sometimes, this may mean paying some bills late. Other times, it may mean missing a bill. This can be an extremely stressful situation, but it requires careful, clear-headed thinking.

Part of making this short-term plan involves understanding the consequences of delaying the payment of certain bills. Once you realize you are going to have to pay a bill late, call your creditors to make short-term arrangements. Do not ignore them, because ignoring them generally makes the problem worse for you.

Risks of paying a bill late are:
• Accruing late fees

- Receiving a negative mark on your credit (which we cover in the next section on credit)
- Getting an increase in your interest rate
- The cancelling of no or low-interest promotions that once applied to the account
- Account closure

While those are all less than ideal scenarios, you can recover from them with a proper plan.

In the meantime, I have created a hierarchy of payments to help you determine what to pay.

FOOD & MEDICINE

HOUSING COSTS

TRANSPORTATION

UTILITIES

DEBT PAYMENTS

EVERYTHING ELSE

Budgeting as a Couple

You know the childhood rhyme, "...first comes love, then comes marriage, then comes the baby in the baby carriage"? Well, they forgot to include a line about managing money as a couple. Money can greatly impact your relationship. It's no wonder that approximately 35 percent of divorcees cite money woes as the primary reason for their irreconcilable differences..

Managing money solo has its challenges, but managing money as a couple can be even more challenging. It doesn't have to be all bad. It really is what you make it. And for people who need accountability, your romantic partner can become one of your greatest allies on your journey to financial freedom.

Since this is not a relationship book, I won't go into the nuisances of talking money with your partner, but I will cover the different ways to manage your money as a couple.

Keep in mind, there is no right or wrong way to manage money as a couple. There will be plenty of advice from your elders and other couples on how to manage your money. A great deal of it will come from experience and a good place. But your relationship is unique and so is your family dynamic. Do what works for you, but WORKS is the important word here. If you're not doing anything to manage your money as a couple, here are a few money management and budgeting options to consider:

All In

With this budgeting strategy, all money earned goes into one account or accounts that you and your partner both have access to. You spend out of this account and pay bills from this account. All In makes budgeting more complex because you must account for each other's expenses along with the household's expenses. There's one overall household budget, and it would likely be more pages than the typical budget since it factors in expenses for two people and those who may depend on them.

Together Apart

Using this particular method, you budget as a household and allocate enough money from your individual income to the household account. In this budget, you also maintain your individual funds—which are budgeted separately. Essentially, you have two budgets: household and personal.

Under this method you don't have to ask for permission or check in with your partner when planning a purchase, but you also don't have the accountability you'd have with the All-In method.

Separate

This budgeting strategy keeps everything completely separate. While you may be responsible for some household items and maintain a household budget on paper, you and your partner would maintain separate accounts. There wouldn't be any co-mingling of funds. When paying household bills, you may split the responsibilities so one person pays the cable, electricity, and insurance while the other person pays the rent or mortgage.

These are three of the most common budgeting types for couples, but there are other ways to effectively manage money as a couple based on changing needs, including employment status, family dynamic, and life events.

Electronic Budgeting vs. Good Ole Paper and Pencil

I'm often asked how to budget and whether or not using electronic software or programs is better than using good ole paper and pencil. What matters most is the fact that you're budgeting.

Your budgeting method really comes down to a matter of preference.

Digital budgeting typically takes on the other formats but is conducted electronically or with the use of budgeting apps or programs. These programs often connect to the owner's account information and segment spending as it occurs, giving the account owner a greater understanding of how much they are spending towards each allocated budget category.

It could also be as simple as a Microsoft Excel spreadsheet with the monthly budget, in which you enter line items and update the spreadsheet regularly. This budgeting method is convenient and can easily be managed on the go. It is important to keep in mind that technology isn't always perfect. It is also helpful to double check your numbers regularly to make sure the system is working in the way you intended.

Paper and pencil budgeting means you write out everything on paper rather than depending on technology to keep track of your spending. This method does require more mindfulness, which in turn might allow you to be more connected with your money.

Helpful Tip: One of the most helpful things you can do is create a bill calendar which sends reminders of impending pay dates. This could be your electronic calendar, your work/home office calendar, or a paper calendar like the one found in the Financial Success Planner.

By creating a bill calendar, you can set reminders for important pay dates so you aren't caught off guard by any of your financial responsibilities.

Budgeting

Managing your money is and should be an active process. Ater all, it's YOUR money. If you don't mind your own business, who will mind it for you?

Credit

I find that most people, in starting their financial journey, are often interested in starting with their credit. I left credit as our last topic for a variety of reasons. I will not dispute the importance of credit and how valuable a financial tool it is, but credit is often an indicator of your overall financial health. Meaning, it isn't the solution to improving your financial situation.

In short, credit is about your relationship to debt and how you manage your debt. It is possible to have bad credit, yet a strong financial foundation because you have a minimal-to-nonexistent amount of debt and adequate savings. It is also possible to have good or excellent credit, yet a rocky financial foundation because you do not have adequate savings and have acquired a large amount of debt.

Credit scores and reports are one of the primary tools lenders use to determine how responsible you are. All your financial history is measured and weighed, enabling the credit bureaus to assign a score to your report for lenders to utilize.

Credit is essential in buying items, particularly big-ticket items. As a society, we're obsessed with buying things, hence the continued references regarding credit scores and the high value we place on credit ratings. While credit isn't everything, it is important because credit is equivalent to your adult GPA.

Chapter 5

Now, let's dig into credit.

We won't go through the history of credit cards, but as a financial product, they are relatively young. Credit cards, as we know them today, are a little more than 50 years old. This means, Generation X grew up during the time when credit cards became prominent, and millennials and Generation Z have never known a world without them.

The most commonly used scoring model is the Fair Isaac Corporation (FICO). There are three major bureaus which create credit reports using the FICO score. They are Experian, Transunion, and Equifax. While all creditors don't report to all these credit bureaus, creditors typically refer to at lease one of these bureaus when making decisions about your creditworthiness.

Although the FICO score is the most popular and Experian, Equifax, and Transunion are the most utilized credit reporting bureaus, it is estimated that each person over the age of 18 will have more than 40 different types of credit score within their adulthood life. This is because FICO is an algorithm, but so are the other scores such as the Vantage Score that we are less familiar with, which all make assumptions regarding the kind of customer we are based on our habits. Insurance companies, mortgage lenders, auto acceptance corporations, and other companies have a stake in our financial responsibility and use information associated with our social security numbers to determine whether or not they'd lend to us.

In this book, the FICO score will be used as our reference point since it is the most widely accepted score. However, you should always ask your lender what information they are using to determine your creditworthiness.

When building credit, the most important point to remember about credit is your relationship to debt and how responsible you are with debt owed and credit lent.

Credit scores range from 300 TO 850

Excellent Credit = 750+

Good Credit = 700 - 749

Fair Credit = 650 - 699

Poor Credit = 600 - 649

Bad Credit = Below 599

These tiers tend to change slightly with economic ratings and standings. During the recession of 2008, people lost their jobs and homes, which affected credit ratings. If you were in the 700s during that time, you were doing pretty good. But due to the recession, lending standards became more strict; a reaction which often takes place following recessions. It's a cycle. When things are good, banks relax and lend money more readily. When things aren't going so well, banks pull back and exercise more caution in lending.

Credit

The following factors make up your credit score:

Payment History (35 percent)

Most people are familiar with this measure, but it is only 35 percent of your total score. Consistent on-time payments improve your score. Late payments, delinquent or over-limit accounts, bankruptcies, and liens significantly lower your score.

Pay on time, all the time, if you can. Remember, a minimum payment is better than a missed payment.

Debt-to-Credit Ratio or Utilization (30 percent)

This is the silent but major factor most people overlook. Also referred to as the "utilization" or revolving utilization, this factor is specific to your overall credit profile and individual credit card accounts. It is suggested you only use 30 percent of the credit available to you on an individual card. For example, if your credit limit is $1,000, you don't want to have a balance of more than $300 on the card because creditors look poorly on consumers who have a heavy reliance on credit (without the ability to pay the balance as often as possible).

I know it sounds like the ultimate set up; you are extended credit and encouraged to use it, but credit bureaus adjust your usage and lower your score if you use all the credit available to you.

At the end of this chapter, there will be an activity to help you fully understand credit utilization by writing down all your open credit accounts, their current limits, and your target utilization.

When it comes to utilization, remember to keep your total revolving utilization ratio as low as possible – 30 percent is good, but 20 percent is better. If you really want to maximize your credit score, aim to keep your revolving utilization at 10 percent or less.

This formula applies to both your total revolving utilization and each individual credit card. Meaning, the sum of all your credit card debt should be 30 percent of all the credit available to you.

For example, if you have a store card with a $500 limit, a travel rewards card with a $3,000 limit, and another card with a $1,500 limit, your sum of credit card debt should not exceed $1,500 when all three balances are combined.

Length of Credit History (15 percent)

The longer you've responsibly used credit, the better. You have to remember credit ratings are all about assessing your risk as a borrower. If you have a proven record of responsibly managing your lines of credit for years, lenders are more likely to lend to you. The longer your credit history, the better. So, avoid closing accounts which have been opened longer, even if you don't use them.

This is why they say no credit is worse than bad credit. If a lender doesn't know how you've managed debt in the past, they don't know how you'll handle potential debt in the future.

New Credit Accounts and Inquiries (10 percent)

Any time you apply for a new line of credit (and it is reported to the credit bureaus), it is called an inquiry. Inquiries indicate to creditors you are shopping around for credit. Credit inquiries remain on your credit report for two years but are only factored into your credit score for the first 12 months.

Applying for a lot of credit in a short period of time can lower your score because it signals to creditors you might be relying on credit or could potentially take on more debt than you can properly manage. Avoid new credit applications if you are planning a major purchase such as a home.

Diversity of Credit (10 percent)

All credit isn't the same. There are two types of credit available to you: revolving and installment.

Revolving credit has no set monthly payment and varies based on your credit usage. Credit cards are a prime example of revolving credit. While credit cards are useful for building credit, lenders also want to see you can manage other types of credit.

Installment credit is typically extended for bigger ticket items, such as homes, vehicles, or education. The payments don't vary and typically remain the same throughout the life of the loan.

Note: While judgments and collection items aren't credit, they negatively affect your score because they indicate you did not responsibly manage financial obligations in the past.

To Use or Not to Use a Credit Card

Few financial tools invoke the fear credit cards do. Credit cards are controversial because they can be hurtful as well as helpful. When used responsibly, credit can be a credit building tool and a flexible resource for expenses, such as refundable deposits and reimbursable business expenses. When used irresponsibly, credit cards can lead to a deep ditch of debt that is difficult to dig out of successfully.

If you are going to use credit cards, it is important to understand the common myths as well as the pros and cons of credit cards so they don't derail your financial goals.

You Don't Need a Credit Card

Credit cards are not a necessity. Credit cards are a tool. Assuming credit cards are a necessity upholds the notion that you cannot survive without borrowing from banks and lenders.

Just keep in mind, if you choose not to utilize credit cards, there are often restrictions on debit card use. For example, hotels and rental car companies may put a hold on your debit card for the full amount until the transaction is complete, ultimately affecting your available cash during a trip.

You Don't Need a Credit Card to Build a Credit Score

Although credit cards are one of the easiest ways to build credit, credit cards are not the only way to build your credit or improve your credit score.

You can build credit by:

- Becoming an authorized user on a relative or spouse's credit card in good standing. The 30 percent utilization rule applies here, along with payment history. You can do bad all by yourself, so make sure the card is in good standing before you get added as an authorized user.

- Using a credit building loan program through a local credit union or company. (A Google search of "Credit Building Loans" is the best way to find companies or banks near you offering this alternative. Just make sure you do your research on their trustworthiness before you enter into a loan program.)

- Paying installment loans (loans with a regular payment for a fixed period), such as car loans, student loans, and mortgages. Paying the required amounts on time will count towards your credit history and improve your credit score.

Fixing errors on your credit report. Errors are prevalent in credit reports and you shouldn't be punished because of an erroneous entry on your credit report. Review your reports from the three major credit bureaus quarterly to ensure accuracy.

Just remember, there comes a point where you have fixed everything you can and will need credit to build credit. You can't "repair" your way to good credit since your credit score is based on your responsible usage of credit.

The Benefits of Using Credit Cards:

- Grace periods to pay for charges
- Protection for fraudulent transactions and ID Theft
- Earn rewards or cash back on certain cards
- Use to build credit score

The Drawbacks of Using Credit Cards:

- Reduces the 'pain' of transactions which can lead to increased spending
- Masks overspending with grace periods
- Interest payments add to overall costs
- Interest rates are high (average 15 percent +)
- Rewards incentives encourage additional spending not saving
- Late payments and high utilization rates can significantly reduce your credit score

*A cash back reward, or miles, is an incentive to spend, whereas a 401k match, for example, is an incentive to save.

Credit cards should not be used as a replacement for adequate savings and proper planning.

What If You're Late on Your Payments?

Things happen. And as good as your intentions may be, there is a chance you could miss a payment on one of your open lines of credit whether unintentionally because of your forgetfulness or on purpose because you didn't have the money to pay the bill due to unexpected expenses (like car repair, doctor visit, etc.).

And we typically wouldn't care if we missed a payment if it didn't affect our credit scores. But we know all too well it can.

An important point to note about a late payment is it won't immediately impact your credit the day after you miss your payment. For example, if you are one day late on a credit card payment, you'll be charged a late fee, but the company isn't going to report it to the credit bureau. Your late payments only report your lateness to your credit bureau when the item is 30 days past due. Once the late payment is reported to your credit bureau it will damage your credit score but the act of being late won't.

If you don't have a history of requesting that late fee transactions be removed, you could also contact the issuer to find out if they would waive the fee this time. This is typically offered as a courtesy and only exercisable every 6 to 12 months.

But, My Credit is Terrible

Bad credit can happen to good people. There is no disputing that having access to credit can make life easier. Good credit allows you makes major purchases more feasible and accessible, and allows you to borrow money easily. Bad credit on the other hand is expensive. If you have bad credit you tend to pay more money in interest because your interest rates are higher. So what do you do when you've used credit poorly in the past?

Should You Hire Someone to Fix Your Credit?

Credit repair is big business. You'd likely have an easier time finding a credit repair specialist than a financial advisor but you don't need to hire someone to repair your credit. It is a matter or preference and convenience.

During the repair process, a credit repair specialist does the following three things:

1) disputes items deemed inaccurate on your credit

2) advises you on what trade lines you should open to build your credit

3) provides you with a forecast of what you'd likely qualify for based on your credit.

These specialists are not paid because they are doing something you can't do, like doctors and lawyers are. They are being paid because disputing items on your credit reports can be time consuming and confusing if you don't have the right resources available to you.

Credit repair can be a specific and lengthy process and for that reason I will not cover it in this book. However, if you have pulled your credit report and your score needs a little work, I highly suggest How to Repair Your Credit by my good friend Dominique Brown. I regularly recommend this book. Dominique is an expert in this field, and he owns a credit repair business where he created a program to help people who can't afford his services gain access to his expertise.

First step, access your credit report (also called pulling your report). You'll need to familiarize yourself with the items on your report to understand what is helping and what is hurting your credit score.

Accessing Your Credit

In order to understand where you are, you'll need to access your credit report, commonly referred to as "pulling" your credit report. You can access your credit report online or you can mail each of the bureaus with copies of your identification (the mail process takes a long time and I highly recommend you access it online).

When you pull your credit report online, you have several options when it comes to accessing it. You can go through your lender (your credit card company), your bank, a service such as Credit Karma or Quizzle, or directly from FICO, the creator of the most commonly used credit score.

I have included resources you can use to gain access to your credit report in the resources section of this book.

In Closing

Your credit is part of your financial foundation, but not your entire financial picture. Keeping your debt to a minimum and responsibly using credit improves your credit rating, which reduces the interest rates you are charged to borrow money.

ADDITIONAL FINANCIAL MATTERS

Now that we've covered the basic elements of your financial foundation, I want to cover what I affectionately call, "the other stuff." They are no less important than the elements covered in-depth in this book, BUT in the interest of keeping things digestible and to the point, I'll only cover them briefly.

If you have additional questions regarding the information in this section or anywhere in this book, I encourage you to seek out additional qualified resources covering the specific subject in question.

Student Loans

Over 40 million people have student loans. Largely touted as a "good debt," millions of students acquired student loan debt in pursuit of their dream of economic security only to graduate into a competitive job market saturated with college graduates and stagnant wages. As a result, people from all socioeconomic backgrounds are feeling the pinch of student loan debts, often having borrowed more than their degree was actually worth.

This section is not a comprehensive guide on navigating your student loans, but hopefully it addresses some of the more common student loan questions you may have.

Chapter 6

There are two types of student loans available: Public and Private.

Public loans, which are commonly referred to as federal loans, are funded by the federal government.

Private student loans are nonfederal loans, made by a lender (i.e., a bank, a credit union, a state agency or school). Private loans are based on creditworthiness. Most federal loans are available for undergraduate and graduate students enrolled in at least six credits regardless of creditworthiness. PLUS loans (Graduate Plus and Parent Plus loans) are the only federal loans whose eligibility is based on creditworthiness.

If you borrowed student loans throughout your collegiate career, there is a possibility you'll need to consolidate your student loans. Consolidation means you're combining your student loans into a single loan.

Whether or not you consolidate is up to you. There are advantages to consolidation like making a single monthly payment to pay off your loan. There are also potential disadvantages of loan consolidation. It is difficult to give a definitive answer as each individual is unique with varied circumstances.

Students who have federal loans can consolidate their loans through the following servicers:

- Great Lakes Educational Loan Services
- Nelnet
- FedLoan Servicing (PHEAA)
- Navient (formerly Sallie Mae)

Private loans cannot be consolidated into a consolidated federal loan, but federal loans can be consolidated into a private loan. I discourage this option because there are a number of benefits with federal loans that include access to forgiveness programs and more lenient repayment options. If you consolidate a federal loan into a private loan, you lose those benefits.

Private loans are eligible for consolidation through various servicers:

- Chase
- NextStudent
- Student Loan NetWork
- Wells Fargo

Each servicer has differing terms and has a cap on the amount of debt you can consolidate. Avoid any lender that charges prepayment fees!

Before consolidating, take your budget and extenuating circumstances into account.

What If You Default on Your Student Loans?

Your student loan is considered "in default" when you have not made any payments for 270 days (nine months) and have not made any arrangements with your servicer.

Defaulting on your student loans adversely affects your credit score. If you have defaulted on your student loans, contact your loan servicer immediately and ask what you need to do to remove your loan from default status. You will be provided with one of the following options for getting your loan out of default.

Loan Repayment

Pay your loan in full. Chances are if your loan is in default, you won't be able to take advantage of this opportunity unless you've come into a windfall of money. Since this isn't a viable option for most of us, you should try to negotiate a monthly repayment plan, such as loan rehabilitation.

Loan rehabilitation plans vary based on the types of loans you have including the following:

- For a Direct Loan, you must make at least nine full payments in the agreed upon amount within 20 days of the monthly due date to the U.S. Department of Education (DOE) for a consecutive nine-month period. Once you have made the nine payments, your loan(s) will be returned to loan servicing.Wage and tax garnishments will not be counted toward your nine qualifying payments.

- For a Federal Family Education Loan, the same guidelines apply to you as they did with a Direct Loan. The difference is once you have made nine payments, an eligible institution may purchase your loans.

- For a Perkins Loan, you must make at least nine on-time monthly payments. Once you have made the required payments, your loan(s) will continue to be serviced by the DOE until the balance owed is paid in full.

Once your loans have been rehabilitated, your monthly payments will probably increase and collection costs may be added to your principal balance.

For more resources on understanding your student loans, please refer to the resources page at the end of the book.

Purchasing a Car

Buying a new car can be exciting and terrifying. After all, you want to make the right choice because this single purchase will most likely impact your finances significantly. Even though people purchase cars daily, the process doesn't come with a decision-making manual (though it should!) and, because of this, most people don't get the best deal when they walk off the lot.

I know because I spent an entire year selling cars during college, and I have purchased several cars over the course of my life.

Before purchasing a car, you should ask yourself the following:

What are the additional costs of ownership?

Although the average vehicle is not as expensive as a home, it is still a major financial decision which impacts you for years, regardless of whether the vehicle is financed or paid in full. You'll likely be responsible for fuel, parking fees, insurance, licensing, registration, routine maintenance such as oil changes and brakes, and more.

Taking this into consideration, you should calculate the foreseeable additional costs such as insurance, repairs, etc., and factor them into your budget. Contact your auto insurance company and request a quote based on the vehicle you are interested in purchasing. Once you have this information, make sure you have sufficient income to cover the additional costs that accompany your car payment.

Should I lease or buy?

Although some people call leasing a vehicle a waste of money, similar to renting versus buying a home, both options have advantages and disadvantages. When it comes to your next car purchase, it's not about which disadvantage list is shorter, it's all about your lifestyle and financial goals.

If you are the type of person who likes to get a new car every three years or whenever the body style changes, leasing might be best for you. The monthly payments will likely be less with a lease. In addition, most consumers never finish paying off an auto loan. They trade in their vehicle long before it is paid off because they want a newer model, need more space, or no longer want to maintain the car. But trading in a car with a balance is how you build negative equity often referred to as being "upside down" in relation to a loan.

Negative equity occurs when an unpaid balance from a previous loan is rolled over into a new loan. Ultimately, you're not only paying for the current car loan, you're also paying off the balance of the previous loan. If you continue to do this, eventually you'll owe more than your car is worth.

If you are not comfortable getting the repairs often needed on an older car you should consider leasing.

If you take frequent road trips or drive often, purchasing might be best for you. This is because when you lease, you have a limited number of miles in your lease contract, typically 12,000 to 15,000 miles a year. If you drive more, you'll have to pay an excess mileage penalty of 10 cents to as much as 25 cents for every additional mile. Unfortunately, if you drive too little, you don't get credited for the unused miles.

Whether your goals are explicitly outlined or implicit, it is likely that you wish to accomplish them within certain time frames. Your financial decisions determine the success of your current and prospective goals. It's important to understand how major financial purchases such as purchasing a car or a home affect your short and long term goals.

Buying a Home

Home ownership is a major life decision requiring adequate financial preparation. Purchasing a home has its benefits, but it isn't for everyone.

If you are an adult who pays rent, you have probably felt pressure from your loved ones and members of your

social circle to "stop throwing your money down the drain and purchase a home."

Though purchasing a home is often touted as a sound investment, research has shown, in most cases, real estate values barely outpace inflation. A home becomes a valuable return on investment if your equity (the amount owed on the home) is less than the market value of the home or if you use it to generate excess income (buying a two-family home and allowing the tenant to pay the mortgage while you live rent free) or an aggressive paying of the mortgage to force equity.

Regardless of your housing decision, you should aim to spend no more than 20 to 30 percent of your take home pay on housing although that is becoming increasingly difficult in today's housing market . As a homeowner, you will also need to account for insurance, taxes, and fees. While mortgage simulators may project homeownership is within your budget, you also want to calculate the additional costs associated with owning your dream home. Determine if you are still within the suggested percentages after the additional expenses are factored into the cost of the home.

Another factor you'll want to consider is length of time you will live in the home. If you are not ready to commit to a city, you might be better off renting until you find a city you can settle in. You could lose money by buying a home and reselling it too quickly because you haven't allowed equity to build. In order to cover the expenses associated with selling, your home needs to appreciate a minimum of 10 percent from the time you purchased it.

Aside from the down payment, here are some additional costs to take into consideration when buying a home:

Earnest Money

Once you find a house you love and decide to submit a contract to purchase the home, you submit earnest money along with the contract to show good faith. The purpose of earnest money is to discourage potential buyers from making simultaneous offers on multiple properties just to "weigh their options." The amount of earnest money needed varies by state and housing market.

For example, in a slower housing market $500 to $1,000 might be sufficient; however, if the owner is receiving multiple inquiries about the property, you might need to make a larger deposit closer to two to three percent of the offer price.

The good thing about earnest money is your deposit goes towards the purchase price of the home if the offer is accepted.

In order to protect your deposit from potential scams, confirm you will receive a receipt and make the deposit payable to a reputable third party—a well-known real estate brokerage, legal firm, escrow company, or title company.

Mortgage Reserve

Another commonly overlooked financial component of the home buying process is the financial reserve. Your financial reserves are accessible liquid assets you can access after the mortgage closes, if needed. While all lenders don't require proof of additional accessible assets on hand, some do. It's best to plan ahead so you aren't denied the loan for your dream home. Reserve requirements vary from bank to bank. Mortgage reserves demonstrate your ability to maintain sufficient amounts of income outside of your typical mortgage payment should you encounter a difficult financial spot, such as job loss or a medical emergency.

Inspection Fees

We've all seen the home repair shows, everything is going fine with the renovation and then bam, an electrical or structural issue demands repairs and demolishes the budget. Homes are complex structures and, despite the curbside appeal and magazine-worthy renovations, everything might not be what it seems. All mortgage insurers do not require a home inspection before closing, but they are recommended for homebuyers.

According to the U.S. Department of Housing and Urban Development, a typical home inspection costs $300 to $500 and varies based on size and location. An inspection is important because existing homeowners might not be forthcoming about issues with the home, or they might not be aware. A few hundred dollars spent on an inspection can give you, the buyer, peace of mind. It can also save you thousands of dollars in repairs in the long run.

Closing Costs

Upon the closing of your home, you will be responsible for closing costs, which are unavoidable fees occurring when the home is transferred from the seller to the buyer. These costs are not factored into the price of your home and are charged in addition to the housing price to cover items including (but not limited to): notary services, title company search fees, attorney expenses, real estate transfer taxes, insurance premiums, and more. Closing costs vary state to state but can range two to five percent of the entire home purchase. You're expected to have the funds to pay for these expenses on the day of closing. The advantage is, the bulk of closing costs are negotiable. They may be paid in part by the seller, and you can shop around for lenders who offer incentives in the form of lower fees at closing.

Moving In

Frequently forgotten, but extremely important, are moving costs. These costs will vary based on circumstances, but even a move across town can be costly. If you're relocating from another home or apartment, you'll likely hire a company or rent a large truck to move your items. Chances are you'll also stock your pantry and refrigerator and purchase cleaning supplies, new furniture, new décor, and other household items to make your house a home.

Maintenance Costs

In an ideal world, your home would be perfect and would remain perfect resisting wear, tear, and environmental damage. The reality is, homes require maintenance and upkeep. The older your home, the more work you'll likely be responsible for over time. Unlike renting, it's your responsibility to repair issues, and you'll need to ensure you have the resources on hand to deal with any unexpected costs or emergencies. This is not just an investment in your sanity, it's also the responsible protection of one of your most valuable assets.

When Does It Make Sense to Rent?

These are the scenarios in which it makes sense to rent:

- If your credit score and credit history aren't strong enough to qualify for a competitive interest rate
- If you are not sure you want to remain in the same city and are uninterested in becoming a landlord
- If you are uninterested in homeownership and the responsibility that comes along with it

When Does It Make Sense to Buy?

These are the circumstances in which it makes sense to purchase a home:

- When buying actually does save you more money
- When you have a stable lifestyle and want the stability homeownership offers
- You want to secure a mortgage at an affordable price before the cost of living in your community becomes unaffordable

Purchasing a home is an exciting experience that can yield dividends for years to come. But it can become riddled with anxiety if you don't take time to assess whether or not homeownership fits into your financial goals.

Taxes

Almost everyone is required to file taxes, but very few people fully understand them.

Tax season begins in January, and it takes into account the year prior to the current year. For example, the 2017 tax season begins in 2018 since there's a chance you earned income up until December 31st of the previous year. You file your taxes with the federal government. Depending on where you reside, you might also file your taxes with the state government. At the time this book was written, the federal government began accepting electronically-filed tax returns around the second week of January.

The deadline to file your taxes—or request an extension—typically falls on a day in the third week of April. If you know you aren't going to meet the filing deadline, you can file an extension; however, the extension request must be submitted by April 18th.

If you are granted an extension, your deadline to file is typically extended through October.

Who Is Required to File a Tax Return?

By law, if you are under age 65, then you are required to file a tax return if:

- You are single and earned more than $10,500
- You are the head of household and earned more than $13,050
- You are married and filing jointly and earned over $20,300 combined
- You are married and filing separately and have earned $3,950
- You are a widow or widower and have earned $16,350 or more

The income limits are for the previous year only a.k.a. the year prior to the current year. You can't add or subtract from three years prior to avoid paying taxes in the current year. Also know that it is possible your filing status can change each year, depending on your income for a given year.

If you are collecting unemployment, you may be required to file taxes.

If you are working a part-time job you may be required to file taxes.

If you are a teenager and claimed as a dependent, you are still required to file taxes (if you meet the income guidelines).

Think about it this way, filing taxes is about your income and not so much about your employment status or age, although different laws apply to people over age 65.

If this information is still confusing, have a look at your paystub. If taxes were deducted from your paycheck throughout the year, then file your taxes to be on the safe side.

In order to file your taxes, you will need the following information:

Social security numbers and birth dates for yourself and your spouse, if married

Social security numbers and birth dates of dependents, if you are claiming them

Depending on your situation, you will need the following documents:

- W-2 forms from each employer you worked for the previous year
- The 1098 form if you are a homeowner.
- The 1098- E if you are paying back student loans
- The 1099 MISC if you earned more than $600 working freelance or independently
- The 1099K if you operate a business and received payments via credit card from third party sites like Amazon or PayPal
- Forms that report your investment income such as the 1099 Dlv, B, &G
- Information regarding any alimony received
- Rental property income/expense information
- Information regarding income from the sale of property
- Information about other miscellaneous income such as jury duty earnings and gambling winnings.

Now, let's discuss how to address life events and changes from the previous year.

If you recently had a baby or adopted a child, you qualify for additional tax benefits. To receive your child tax credit, simply indicate the change in the dependent section of your tax form when you file the taxes. Also, remember you will need to provide the social security numbers and birth dates of the dependents you are claiming.

If you have assumed responsibility of caring for a parent, they may also be considered a dependent if you provide more than 51 percent of their support costs, such as food, housing or lodging, clothing, and medical services and/or equipment.

If you were recently married, you have the option of filing jointly or separately. Your marital status on December 31st determines whether you are considered married for the year of filing. According to the IRS, couples should choose the filing status that is best for them. The tax law allows married couples the choice of filing their federal income tax return either jointly or separately in any given year. This means you could file jointly one year and separately the next year.

Determine which filing status will result in the lowest tax owed. Traditionally, filing jointly is more beneficial, but filing separately has its benefits if you don't want to factor your spouse's income into your income. For example, if you file jointly, your spouse's income is taken into consideration when calculating how much you can afford to pay monthly towards your student loans.

If you have moved since the last tax season, you qualify for a tax credit to offset your moving expenses. Don't forget to contact your current and former employers and inform them of your address change so you can receive your documents at your current address. Also, make sure you notify the U.S. Postal Service when you move so they can forward any IRS correspondence or refunds. This step is important for receiving mail, period.

No matter how small the amount you think you have earned this past year, you still might be required to file taxes.

It is best to speak with a tax professional to find out if you should file, rather than assume you aren't required to file.

While there are several sites (and different software) that make it easy to self file, I highly encourage individuals who have complex financial situations, their own businesses, or a lack of confidence in effectively filing themselves, to hire a tax professional.

Creating A Legacy, Not Liabilities

So, what is this all really for? Why are we pursuing financial freedom? What is the goal?

Often, our desire to be financially secure extends beyond our own short-term desires. The greater goal is to establish a legacy so future generations don't have to struggle. Research shows that one of the leading contributors to the wealth disparity gap between blacks and white are gifts and inheritances. This money can be used to jumpstart more wealth accumulation, such as purchasing real estate, investing, or starting a business.

Yet, despite our desire to leave a legacy, many people leave liabilities.

One of the easiest ways to improve the financial future of those who directly depend on you is to set a good money example.

Your children are watching you. Often, what you do will impact them more than what you say. The relationship you have with money can shape your children's perspective and experience. Helping your children inherit a healthy relationship with money is invaluable. The more responsible you are with your money, the better your relationship becomes with money, allowing you to instill money management confidence early on instead of the fear most children inherit from financially-insecure parents.

One of the greatest gifts a parent can give their children is financial security. In the absence of financial insecurity, your children can focus on their dreams and establish a strong foundation for their household rather than financially support you, their parent. This doesn't mean they wouldn't emotionally support you or take care of you in the event of the unforeseen, but it means you won't become a financial burden.

If you are closer to financial security and are seeking to do more with your expendable income, you can establish a

Roth IRA for your child. Currently, parents can contribute $5,500 to a Roth IRA if they are under age 50. Parents can contribute $6,500 if they are over the age of 50. Parents are able to make withdrawals on their contributions (not earnings) from Roth IRA accounts prior to age 59 ½ without incurring a tax penalty, as long as the money is used for higher education expenses.

The money will accumulate tax free just like it would in a 529 plan. However, if the child doesn't go to college, gets a full scholarship, or pays for school some other way, then the money will stay in the Roth. It can be used for a down payment on a house, for disability, or to jumpstart a parent's retirement savings.

Another way to pass on wealth is to buy stock for the young people in your life.

According to Fidelity, the U.S. stock market has consistently earned more than bonds over the long term, despite regular ups and downs in the market. With new companies going public every day, purchasing stock as a gift could be a sound investment that becomes a valuable investment over time. You can set up a custodial account and ask for cash as birthday gifts (for your children) to purchase stock—in some of their favorite companies—on their behalf. It is a gift that keeps on giving, even after trends have expired and your children lose interest in toys.

Lastly, consider purchasing a life insurance policy.

While some experts are against it, life insurance could be a valuable asset for parents who are asset poor. If you contribute to the financial well-being of another human being, it's safe to say you need life to protect your family against the financial impact of losing you.

Term life and whole life insurance are two types of policies widely available to consumers and the differences are reflected in the cost.
Term coverage is the most affordable life insurance option and provides coverage for the specified timeframe stated in the policy, whether it's 10, 20, or 30 years. The younger you are, the more affordable it is. The policy cost increases as the insured person ages.

Whole Life (a.k.a. universal or permanent policy) acts similar to a term policy wherein a benefit is paid after death, but this type of policy accumulates a cash value. Whole life insurance policies remain in effect for the entire life of the insured and the premiums do not increase with age.

In the event of a premature death, a life insurance policy could replace your financial contributions to the household or enable your children to pay off your mortgage and other liabilities you incurred. Aside from this, a life insurance payout could be used to fund a business or other investments your child might not have the income for otherwise.

Keep in mind, a term life insurance policy is often cheaper, yet it expires after a certain amount of years. For example, if you purchase a 30-year term life insurance policy at 28, the policy will expire at 58, and you will lose all the money you put into the policy. A whole term policy, however, is often slightly more expensive, but does not expire.
Although your employer may offer a life insurance benefit, you should still get a separate policy. The value of your employer's policy is usually your salary, or two times your salary. The industry standard recommendation is that your policy equal 10 to 12 times your salary. This is the suggested standard however most people are covered with a policy that would cover their burial and outstanding bills such as a mortgage. iIt is also important to know that you'll lose coverage if you leave the job unless your employer offers a portable policy. Even so, please note the costs of doing so are often higher than what you would pay if you purchased a separate, independent policy. If you are employed by your job for several years, without an independent policy, you could miss the opportunity to lock in lower rates at a younger age by waiting until you are no longer employed by that company.

There are several other ways to create generational wealth. This is just the start of the conversation. My hope is that you'll expand beyond the suggestions I listed above and find even more ways to contribute to the financial well-being of future generations and those who rely on you.

Finishing Strong and Staying Motivated

In this book, I have covered savings, debt, budgeting, credit, and other financial topics to help you create the best version of your financial self, so you can achieve financial freedom and live a life you love.

Of course, none of this information is useful if you don't implement it. While I don't expect you to be perfect, I ask you to commit to implementing the information shared in this book.

If becoming financially free was easy, everyone would be financially secure, and there would be no need for people like me or the thousands of books written on achieving financial security.

You will encounter obstacles along the way. The best way to overcome these obstacles is to plan for them or seek to avoid them altogether.

Here are a few things you can do to block out the external noise and focus on your financial goals.

Go on a Social Media Fast

Social media has made us more connected than ever,

for better or for worse. Thanks to technology and a few swipes, you're privy to new cars, new hobbies, new homes, new children, new hair, new lip gloss, and anything else people see fit to share or brag about on social media.

Everyone goes to social media to post their highlights, creating an altered sense of reality. If you find yourself competing or becoming dissatisfied with what you have in your life, disconnect for a preselected time frame to focus on the things that make you happy. This disconnection could be for a day, a week, a month, or forever. Life won't cease because of your inactivity on social media, and the (social media) fast may help you be a little more appreciative of everything in your life.

Stay Away from Stores

My mom used to say, "If you go looking for trouble, you'll find it." I once did an experiment and kept myself out of stores for an entire month. Guess what? I spent a significantly less amount of money that month. As a matter of fact, I did not buy one piece of clothing for the entire 30 days.

Marketing firms and departments spend millions of dollars researching consumer habits, so they can create environments encouraging you to spend. (Those "deals" bins near the checkout lines are the devil!)

There is a lot of budget-busting energy being thrown your direction. By staying out of stores, you take the most essential component out of the marketer's equation: YOU. This also includes staying away from online stores. Resist the urge to click through the ad in your news feed or the sidebar of your browser. Focus your energy on the things that will help you make money instead of spending it.

And while you are at it, disable auto-pay. Auto pay makes it easy for stores to collect their money and even easier for you to spend your money.

Lastly, prominently place your financial goals in places where you'll remember them. They'll remind you not to spend. When I was saving money to leave my nine to five job, I frequently asked myself if certain purchases contributed to my financial goal before I made the purchase. If the answer was no, I then asked myself why I was making the purchase since I declared that becoming self-employed was the most important goal in my life during that time.

It's easy to be a hyper consumer. Anyone can spend money, but exceptional people save.

You can buy a designer handbag, but you can't buy an emergency savings account or freedom from debt. Savings and freedom from debt come over time with dedication and commitment. By shifting your focus and energy to the things money can't buy, you remove the power of "stuff" over you.

Your current and future self will thank you for it.

Conclusion

I officially began my own journey to financial freedom in 2013, and my progress hasn't been linear. I've experienced wide stretches of financial success, as well as setbacks, including unpaid invoices, medical emergencies, and debts requiring me to take my own advice. And honestly, that is the spirit with which I share this book. The book was four years in the making. While I became frustrated with each passing year that the book remained unwritten, I realized (with each year) I was learning from students and from my own experiences. All of these experiences helped create the book I wish I had when I started my financial journey.

The road to financial freedom won't always be perfect, and it won't always be easy. There will be moments when you look back on who you were when you started the journey—compared to who you are as a result of the journey—and realize it was worth it.

Resources

On the following pages you'll find services, products, and companies that I use and/or those I know are valuable. While MyFabFinance.com is s complete resource for all of your needs, these resources can support you along your financial journey.

Credit

AnnualCreditReport.com

The Fair Credit Reporting Act (FCRA) requires each of the nationwide credit reporting companies — Equifax, Experian, and TransUnion — to provide you with a free copy of your credit report, at your request, once every 12 months. You can access you reports for free at AnnualCreditReport.com but please note this is only for your credit report and you would have to pay to access your credit score.

MyFico.com Forums

When I began my credit journey I found these forums to be extremely helpful. They were full or real life people dealing with every credit related issues you could think of. I would search these forums before applying for new credit or requesting credit line increases. You can also find out what successes or challenges people had when working with specific creditors.

Local City or State Consumer Agency

Most major cities or states have a consumer service

bureaus that were created to help consumers navigate the legality of collection attempts and to understand their rights. These agencies often provide credit repair resources free of charge to the community.

The Consumer Financial Protection Bureau (CFPB) (Consumerfinance.org)
THe CFPB protect consumers from unfair, deceptive, or abusive practices and take action against companies that break the law. They provide relevant and helpful information, steps, and tools free of charge to any and everyone.

Saving

Digit (digit.co)
People talk about automating your bills, digit automates your savings. It is a savings automation software that connects to your account and based on your account balance and spending habits, automatically saves money for you. I've saved an additional hundred dollars in the past 3 months by using this. It's not a substitute for your regular savings, but a good, easy supplement to help you save even more. Digit charges $2.99 a month for their service. If you would like a free option check out Qapital. com

Trim (Asktrim.com)
Trim pulls in your data, then identifies your subscription payments by finding those that are the same amount, or

nearly the same amount, and billed on a regular basis. The software is smart enough not to pick up things like Starbucks, even if you have a daily latte that always costs the same, though.

After it identifies a consumer's subscriptions, it offers an easy way for you to unsubscribe.

Investing

Stash (stashinvest.com)
Did you know that you can start investing with as little as $5? Investing can seem daunting, but Stash allows you to begin investing on your own without the high minimum opening account balance. With Stash you can learn how to invest yourself. They give you the choices, tools, and tips you need to build a portfolio that reflects who you are. The best thing is you can manage it from your phone. Even if you already have other investment accounts Stash is a good (and cheap) way to diversify your holdings.

Robinhood (Robinhood.com)
Robinhood places the power to invest every day people. They offer free stock trades through its iOS and Android apps, as well as through a web version. As of 2018 the company has more than 3 million users and estimates that users have saved $1 billion since it was created

Acorns (www.acorns.com)
The Acorns app invests your spare change. By rounding up to the nearest dollar (or more) for every credit card purchase and micro-invests the difference. It makes saving fun and easy. On the downside, the increments are probably two small to be effective for long-term savings.

Healthcare

PolicyGenius (PolicyGenius.com)
Shopping for life insurance doesn't have to be hard. Policy Genius has taken all of the confusion out of this very process and makes it easier to provide for your family and those you care about the most. If people depend on you, you need life insurance. Receive a free estimate now to find our how inexpensive protecting your legacy actually can be.

Travel

AirBNB (Airbnb.com
An affordable alternative to hotels. You can rent rooms to villas and castle using this popular shared economy site. As a regular traveler, I have found that this is one of the most affordable ways to find reasonable accommodations at my destination city. I've stayed in AirBnB's from Philadelphia to Los Angeles to Puerto Rico and Cartagena, Columbia and enjoy the authentic experience AirBnb hosts afford me.

Tripping.com

The self-proclaimed "world's largest search engine for rentals". Don't just stop at AirBNB. Tripping allows you to quickly compare vacation homes and short-term rentals in 150,000 destinations around the world to find the best deal for your next getaway.

Hopper (www.hopper.com)

Hopper will predict the future price of flights and tells you when to buy. You will put in your desired flight route and dates and the app will notify you when the right time to buy a tickets comes.

Hotel Tonight (Hoteltonight.com)

Sometimes things don't go as planned and you need a room last minute. HotelTonight makes it easy and fast to find you the best deal and it works in over 35 countries.

Wiffinity (Wiffinity.com)

Wi-fi is essential for travelers, or anyone with a smartphone and/or tablet. Wiffinity is an app that allows users to find and easily connect to wi-fi networks worldwide.

Acknowledgements

Sharon and Joseph Rapley. Your military service laid the groundwork for my education, my work ethic, my commitment to integrity, and my freedom to become the woman and business owner I was created to be. Thank you for your service and unyielding love and support. I've always wanted to make you proud, and this book is a testament to the wonderful job you did as parents. Thank you for your continued support and the money lessons you taught me; the money lessons that allowed me to build my own financial house.

Nicole Rapley. I honestly don't think I'd be the woman I am if it weren't for you. Thank you for talking me out of quitting My Fab Finance the weekend in Atlantic City when I was in a valley and couldn't see my purpose clearly. Thank you for coming up with the name for this business and for being my original accountability partner. Making you proud is a major reason I do what I do.

Khomari Flash, Mr. Fab Finance. We've been together since I started this journey and you've been my trusty companion along the way. From shooting my videos to giving me pep talks when I couldn't see my own power, you are the strong man standing behind this strong woman. Thank you for your selflessness and for allowing me to work those late nights and weekends in pursuit of my dream.

My Friends. There are too many of you to name, but you know how important you are to me. Thank you for showing up to my events, spreading the word about my work, sharing my videos, and getting just as excited as I get (if not more) about my successes. I also want to thank you for praying for me, being petty for me, laughing with me, and celebrating with me. I appreciate you. We got another book, y'all!

Jessica Janniere, my accountability partner during this book journey. Your words during this process motivated and inspired me. I wouldn't have finished this book in a timely matter had it not been for you. I am thankful for you, sister. Thank you for encouraging me to look up and beyond.

My Mastermind Comrades from the Focused Group Family and the True Speaking Success Tribe. It really takes a village and you all were my village during this process. Thank you for answering my questions, conducting informational interviews to help me write this book, and helping me make important book-related decisions when I didn't have it in me.

The My Fab Finance Community. This book is your book. You've allowed me into your lives and we've shared this journey together. Not a day passes that I don't wake up wondering how I can make your lives better or help you along your journey. I thank you all for cheering me along and inviting me into your home and lives. You have given my life a new purpose, and I am forever thankful for you.

CPSIA information can be obtained
at www.ICGtesting.com
Printed in the USA
BVHW061917190820
586728BV00002B/3